THE COLONIZED

And the

Scramble for Africa

Also by Wanjirũ Warama

Unexpected America

Entangled in America

Years of Shame

Beyond Conscious Self

THE COLONIZED

And the

Scramble for Africa

Wanjirũ Warama

Athomi Books

San Diego, California, USA

wanjiruwarama.com

United States of America

Library of Congress Control Number: 2021920593

ISBN: 978-1-954423-04-6

Cover Design by ebooklaunch.com

Published by Athomi Books

8064 Allison Ave, #684, La Mesa, CA, 91942

United States of America

DEDICATION

This book is dedicated to my late parents, Warama wa Njerũ and Mary Nyacuru Ndurumo Warama, who did the best they knew how under very difficult conditions.

TRANSLATION

Gĩkũyũ	Kiswahili	English
Gĩkũyũ	Kikuyu	Tribe or language
Agĩkũyũ	Wakikuyu	Kikuyu people
Mũthũngũ	mzungu	white man.
Mũtũmia mũthũngũ	Bibi Mzungu	A white woman
Memsahib	-	Married or upper class white woman
Athũngũ	wazungu	white people
Ngoi	–	baby carrier
Thabarĩ	safari	Trip, tour, journey
Kĩondo	chondo	woven basket

NOTE: Swahili – popular term; Kiswahili – grammatical term

CONTENTS

Family, Marriages & abuse 119

State of Emergency 201

Sickness & Health

First Author's Note

Stories and events in this book are nonfiction and took place between 1884 and 1956. Except for a few events referenced from historical accounts, the rest were witnessed or experienced by the author and her siblings, her parents, and her community.

Quotations came from the author's recollections, reconstruction, and statements by relatives and others, which she translated from Gĩkũyũ or Kiswahili to English.

The author uses actual names except in a handful of cases where she and her community did not know the individuals' names, or the names proved hard to pronounce, and in time faded from collective memories.

It helps to keep in mind that Kenya, like the rest of Africa, is a complex place with diverse cultures.

This book covers a small part of the author's family and the Gĩkũyũ community.

* * *

Second Author's Note

Is a peasant girl's life worth telling, writing, or reading about?

I, Wanjirũ Warama, asked myself that question many times before and after I started writing this book. After all, I am not famous or known beyond my family and friends. But I was born on a British colonial farm in Kenya where I grew up in the 1950s and 1960s.

Back then, a peasant girl looked forward to nothing more than marriage, motherhood, and farm work.

In Solai, where my family lived on one of the European farms, it was very rare for a girl to attend school. I doubt there was any by 1956. If she did, however, she dropped out or finished her education between grades two and four, the highest level our local schools offered.

To be honest, my only claim to fame is that I started school at least four years late. And, despite that, I beat the odds, meandered through formal and informal education, and attained a graduate degree. And since my twenties, I have involved myself with philanthropy work for my family and others.

I'm especially passionate about education—whether it's from universities, trade or technical schools—because education is one tool that can rescue someone from the debilitating and dehumanizing poverty similar to the one I endured in my teens and early adulthood.

Before the idea of this book took form, I had already written about my American experiences in *Unexpected America* and *Entangled in America*. It, therefore, seemed logical to write about my life and that of my family and community who lived on the colonial farm where it all began.

When I started writing, however, and before the manuscript took shape, my resolve shook. It bothered me to disclose intimate and unpleasant incidents about my family, my Gĩkũyũ tribe, and myself. I got tempted to leave out or glaze over subjects like physical abuse and our pitiful bare minimum existence.

But what was the point if I left out the truth—the ugly, harsh family conflicts?

It eased my mind that my parents—especially my father—were dead and gone, beyond embarrassment and humiliation.

Besides, despite islands of ugliness, I wanted to record my family's and community's oral history and their everyday lives, stories that feature low on society's caste system and hardly appear anywhere in mainstream literature.

My parents grew up with a wealth of authentic Gĩkũyũ (the largest tribe in Kenya) history, untainted by the later

British culture. They also spent decades on a farm owned by a colonizer, where they scratched out a living their entire lives.

Because of vagaries of history, they ended up with dual experiences—one before the British invasion and the other during the occupation.

To put those stories in perspective, my paternal great-grandparents died before they saw a white person, and my grandparents (who may not have met any) died and left minor children early in the twentieth century before the British turned Kenya into a colony in 1920. My family's legacy, therefore, which has shaped my life and that of my siblings, started with my father, Warama wa Njerũ.

Born around 1892, he grew up in Nyĩrĩ (Nyeri), overlooking Mt. Kenya, over twenty-five years before Kenya became a colony. My mother was born about 1910. And despite her growing up at her uncle's homestead on a British farm in Nanyuki, the uncle and the Gĩkũyũ families who lived there still practiced a measure of their traditions.

My parents' knowledge of the Gĩkũyũ tribe, therefore, is based on authentic history, passed down from their ancestors and their community.

But because they never learned to read and write, they and most Kenyans of that era died with most of their stories unrecorded. By default, they "entrusted" outsiders to write about their lives or ignore them altogether.

These incidental trustees, many of them foreigners or locals of a different culture, knew little about our people or the lives we led on those farms. The writers embraced whatever skewed or incorrect information they picked up about us. Sometimes they embellished their writings to fit popular perceptions or outright lied.

As mentioned above, most children who were lucky to attend school in my generation and older reached grade four. That was the highest level of most African schools that the colonial government and missionaries built. These benefactors needed natives (males in particular) educated just enough to perform basic clerical work and record-keeping or to read the Bible. No colonizer wanted well-educated Africans who would develop lofty ideas about their seized lands or human and civil rights.

Thus, few Africans reached a high level of formal education to appreciate writing to preserve their history for future generations. By the time they settled into their colonial reality and started thinking of history, the British and missionaries had already dismantled African institutions—of preserving such records through storytelling and rituals, among others—through outright assault and introduction of their own culture.

As a result, the colonizers—starting with their brethren who first entered the African continent—composed and recorded Kenya's initial written history from their own perspective.

As the Kenya colony matured, European and American journalists and other writers dashed into the country and relied on those colonizers' faulty accounts to feed their readers with memorable stories back in their homelands. The books and newspaper articles they wrote, with an exception of those on wildlife, more than justified colonization. Their general theme excused brutality toward native people as a necessity to civilize the savages and christianize the so-called pagans. Journalists and authors like the late William Zinsser deserve credit. He debunked and apologized for newspaper articles and a book (which he later withdrew) that he wrote during his trip to Kenya. He and his colleagues had fed American readers with page-turner books and articles based on exaggerated or false colonizers' accounts of the Mau Mau freedom fighters.

Even in post-independent Kenya, other authors continued to write using earlier fudged references, mythical beliefs, or lack of knowledge about the natives. In doing so, they sought little input from those indigenous people.

And books written by African academics on Kenya's earlier years relied on the colonial masters' and their supporters' biased records.

But who could blame those authors?

Like the rest of Africans, the writers learned and got molded at an early age by European system of education. They absorbed and internalized skewed textbooks, novels, and newspapers written by Europeans.

African authors (Ngũgĩ wa Thiong'o, Maina Kĩnyattĩ, J.M. Kariŭki, detention camp survivor, and a few others excepted) who could have relied on authentic oral history found it hard to collect information because of lack of know-how, money, or sponsors to support their endeavors.

Facing Mt. Kenya by Jomo Kenyatta is an exception. Despite its extensive record of Gĩkũyũ history and customs, however, readers need to overlook misspelled Gĩkũyũ names and words that, I suppose, Mr. Kenyatta mangled in order to accommodate foreign readers.

Besides, academics and custodians of history did not and still do not put as much weight on oral references as they do on literary ones.

One claim put forward, and which some people still quote, is that the Gĩkũyũ tribe conquered the Athi people unknown centuries ago and took over their lands. To these claimants, this justified the British invasion and seizure of Gĩkũyũ nation's lands.

If western countries applied this argument, Europeans and their descendants would find themselves in quite a mess.

Another reason given, which allegedly caused the British government to sanction the seizure of African lands and establish the "white highlands," swaths of fertile temperate lands they designated for whites only, was because the development of those empty lands went beyond the natives' capabilities.

It is a phony and indulgent excuse for taking people's lands because, in the invaders' opinion, the land seemed idle. The invaders conveniently forgot that they developed the "white highlands" or the so-called empty lands through forced or cheap labor from the displaced natives.

I, for one, do not give credence to most books written by Europeans about the Gĩkũyũ tribe—or about other Africans—before the 1970s, unless the authors based their writings on authenticated anthropology. Even for books published after the 1970s, writers often highlight stories of Kenya that are alien to indigenous people. Below is an example of an excerpt from *I Dream of Africa* by Kuki Gallmann, published in 1991.

> In Kenya, flying in small aircraft is the natural way of getting around, and a popular one since the early days when roads were often non-existent and distances to be covered enormous. Private airstrips are common on farms and ranches, easy to build and to maintain with adequate farm machinery, and there are no complicated procedures to follow. Flying is not regarded as a luxury, but is accepted as an invaluable way of speeding communication, doing business and maintaining friendships. One can literally land in friends' paddocks and walk to their houses for a drink. One can have breakfast on the coast in Lamu, lunch in the Highlands of Laikipia, and dinner by Lake Turkana, a journey which could take weeks by car. ... many people in Kenya fly their own aircraft.

The above quote refers to a country where at least ninety percent of the people have never dreamed of flying and have seen a plane only in the sky.

*

Faced with this kind of misinformation, my timidity faltered. Illiterate people like my parents lacked the ability to record their own stories.

But I do, I told myself.

Why would I then leave it to non-peasants and foreigners to write second-hand, biased, or untrue stories about the peasant life led by my generation?

After all, I still possess the history and the culture my parents passed on to my siblings and me, told in dribbles, with some accounts left out or shielded from our young ears.

I record here how thousands of children, including me, grew up on those British farms in Kenya. Most accounts are what I experienced, saw, heard, and learned from my parents, siblings, neighbors, and others who lived and worked on one of those colonial farms.

But before the personal stories, chapter 1 gives a brief history of the scramble for Africa, which set, fragmented and displaced communities, and changed the course of Africa.

Chapter 1

Scramble for Africa

Before 1884, self-governing micro-nations spread throughout the African continent. The Maasai, the Luo, the Gĩkũyũ, and the Kamba nations (to name just four out of Kenya's 42 tribes) inhabited Kenya that we know of today.

These relatively small nations came from different backgrounds and occupied separate lands. They practiced distinct cultures from foods, languages, legal systems, traditions, legends, and religious myths and superstitions.

For centuries, the nations interacted, traded, and waged wars—mainly raids for livestock—amongst themselves.

But without advanced weapons, they never devastated each other as Asians, Europeans, and other nations did in their homelands.

Then in 1884, European powers' representatives met for a conference in Berlin, Germany. They represented Britain, Germany, France, Belgium, Italy, the Netherlands, and Portugal. They discussed the best way to slice and conquer the African continent that they dubbed "The Dark Continent" because they knew little about it.

Even today, some authors who visit one corner of a single country, out of the 54 African countries and return home to write about "Africa," still use the "Dark Continent" relic.

As Paul Bohannan notes in *Africa and Africans*:

"Africa has for generations now, been viewed through a web of myth so pervasive and so glib that understanding it becomes a twofold task: the task of clarifying the myth and the separate task of examining whatever reality has been hidden behind it. Only as it is stated and told can the myth be stripped away. Only if the myth is stripped away can the reality of Africa emerge."

By the late 1800s, however, Europeans were ready to tackle and unravel the "Dark Continent." Through what they later labeled "The Scramble for Africa," those European men, on behalf of their governments, spread a map on a table and, sight unseen, chopped African communities amongst their countries, like a giant chocolate cake at a party.

A year later, in 1885, they returned to Berlin and formalized their agreement.

Before then, Europeans and others merely trickled to African coasts. But after the Berlin agreement, heralded by the missionaries, they descended on Africa like vultures on roadkill. They quashed one native uprising after another and conquered the micronations. The new conquerors seized lands and established farms where now landless natives flocked in search of employment to enable them to take part in the new cash economy.

Employers expected these natives to work and live with other strangers—members of other tribes—amicably under one colonial law of the land.

The new "owners" brought and enforced cultures from their homelands. These included legal systems, religious heroes, legends, myths and superstitions, monetary systems, and taxation. As a result, the original micronations' systems, now dismantled, stopped evolving and withered.

Today, only tiny slivers of the old systems like marriage intricacies remain embedded in the larger Gĩkũyũ community.

Pre-British invasion, the micro-nations ran intricate governance that would have rivaled any modern religious, social, or legal system, at least with the Gĩkũyũ system.

Why then were they not advanced like the westerners, one would ask?

One major reason was the pleasant climate. The micro-nations had no pressing motivation to tie their existence to imperial tendencies or the desire to grab land and rule over others. They, therefore, had not conquered, formed, and merged lasting alliances or collaborated on a large scale with their neighbors.

For this reason, the micro-nations did not have industrial capitalism or majestic structures before the colonizers descended on them.

The Europeans stripped these micro-nation societies of their autonomy and authority, never to be free of foreign intrusion ever again, even after independence.

According to Daniel Thwaite in *Seething African Pot*, one mistake the European invaders made was to believe they did not need any expertise beyond brute force and literal application of their Bible to draw the boundaries, convert, and govern the natives. They, the conquerors, assumed that to manage and elicit total compliance from the natives required merely less-educated white men.

The assumption was that the less intelligent and educated were mentally closer to the natives and therefore could better preach and interpret the Christian Gospel to evangelize the so-called ignorant savages.

Initially, therefore, the colonies became a dumping and training ground for unsavory and marginal individuals from the bottom rungs of their homeland societies.

To these conquerors, one black skin looked the same as the next. So, when they descended on their spoils and created their new colonies and protectorates, they did not concern themselves with which micro-nation owned what and lived where. They drew arbitrary boundaries and clustered citizens—now termed tribes—together into a hodgepodge of larger countries. The conquerors then split some micronations and even individual families between two countries under different colonial masters.

In Kenya, the British split the Luo nation between Kenya and Uganda, the Maasai between Kenya and Tanzania, and Somalis between Kenya and Somalia.

The Kenya and Somalia split turned out the worst. After Kenya attained independence from Britain on December 12, 1963, Somalia demanded the strip of land that Kenyan

Somalis occupied, intending to unite the formally split community. The disagreement escalated to the *Shifta* War of the 1960s.

Although the war ended without a change in boundaries, the split remains a thorn in Kenya's northern border.

But because of its central location, the Gĩkũyũ nation that occupied temperate climate farmlands around Mount Kenya did not suffer a split. Instead, the British crushed their uprising, torched their homes, killed thousands, and took their goats as war booty. The invaders then seized their lands and crammed the people into a smaller area termed the *native reserve*, similar to the Native American reservations in the United States.

The intruders then apportioned the lands among the various pioneer interest groups. They gave missionaries like the Church of Scotland Mission (CMS) and the Consolata Mission (CM) their portion.

They designated another portion as *White Highlands,* where only whites could live and own land. Africans could live there only as domestic workers or farm laborers. And the rest became Crown Lands under the Crown Lands Ordinance, meaning they now belonged to England.

After they accomplished what the colonizers expected of them, the Indians, who the British had shipped from India to help build Kenya/Uganda railway, got the town centers where they built stores and became shopkeepers.

Initially, Britain designated Kenya as a protectorate in 1895, mainly to protect the missionaries, explorers, and traders from the natives who wanted the intruders out.

With protection, the Kenyan doors opened to all and sundry. Fortune-seekers, speculators, Christian missionaries, charlatans, and hoodlums came to lay claim, make a quick shilling, spread their afterlife beliefs, avoid prosecution, or run from creditors and family entanglements, and start life anew.

Most of the new adventurers bought a one-way steamship ticket—with spare change for a meal—to get to Mombasa, Kenya's largest coastal town.

After the occupiers took most of the natives' lands, they still wanted prime lands where those natives lived. The occupiers weaseled in and manipulated the micronations' leaders with bogus agreements. Some leaders did not fall for the trickery and fights broke afresh. The colonizers quashed those uprisings with disastrous results to the natives.

Some leaders knew their people could not win in combat, but they were too gullible to realize the British would not keep their word. So, they entered into agreements with the British representatives.

One case cited—that I heard about when I was a young girl—is of a Gĩkũyũ leader, Waiyaki wa Hinga. In 1890, he allowed Captain (later Lord) Frederick Lugard to build a post on behalf of the Imperial British East Africa Company (IBEAC) on Gĩkũyũ lands. This was to facilitate building the Uganda-Kenya Railway. The two men took an oath—a solemn pledge to Gĩkũyũ community—that Captain Lugard's use of the land was temporary.

But Captain Lugard did not intend to respect the oath. It did not take long before the relationship soured.

From the community's accounts, his porters looted goats, raped women, harassed, and devastated the Gĩkũyũ community so they would vacate and abandon their lands.

By 1892, relations deteriorated to an extent where, in retaliation, the people burned Lugard's outpost to the ground. The IBEAC representatives arrested Waiyaki wa Hinga and took him to Taita Taveta County, where they buried him upside down and alive in an unmarked grave. The shock and trauma to the Gĩkũyũ community became so deep that they have passed that story on from one generation to the next.

When the colonizers crushed most micro-nations to a point where they could not rise again—besides skirmishes here and there—from Iria rĩa Rũkang'a (Indian Ocean) to Iria rĩa Rũĩgĩ (Lake Victoria), they planned for their new country.

The first item was a railway line to transport goods such as tea, coffee, and pyrethrum (and passengers) from the interior to the coast for shipment or travel to England. They imported cheap labor from India—a British colony at the time—and completed the railway from Mombasa to Kisumu on Lake Victoria in 1901.

The colonizers "upgraded" Kenya to a British colony nineteen years later in 1920.

With the colony under control, the new owners finally organized Kenya under the English power structure. The British as landowners and rulers while Kenyans became British subjects, and grown men, including former heads and pillars of their communities, became mere "boys."

The Royal Crown allocated free land, particularly to ex-military personnel, whereas others paid only cents per acre. Many of these British pioneers became wealthy land barons.

To avoid competition between Christian groups, each religious denomination occupied its own sphere of conversion and indoctrination. My home area of Solai, which my father migrated to in the 1920s when he left Nyeri in search of work, belonged to the Anglicans (Episcopalians). The neighboring Major Stein's farm, where my cousins from my mother's side lived, belonged to the Catholics.

The missionaries throughout Kenya and the rest of Africa remained front and center in converting Africa and turning it into a collection of nations that remain in tribal strife to this day. It's true they benefited the natives with formal education, but those missionaries also maligned and suppressed African religions and traditions, the fabric of a people, including their very existence which they termed backwardness. They replaced them with their form of the so-called "true" God and their version of civilization.

And the colonial administrators enforced British laws and added others on a whim copied from the Draconian slave system in the Americas and apartheid in South Africa.

This book chronicles how my family and other farmworkers and their children lived and navigated through the British colonial system.

Early Memories

Chapter 2

My First Bus Ride

Wawerũ snugged on my back in a *ngoi,* its strap across my tender head. Simon, my fourteen-year-old brother, threw a piece of cloth over the baby and helped me tie it around my chest for reinforcement.

My father and I started early that morning. We needed to catch the only bus that ran between Solai and Nakuru town. He led while I followed for the two miles to the bus stop.

The dew on both sides of the footpath through the savanna remained fresh. It wet my feet, but only for a short distance before we branched into dirt and stunted grass tractor trail, typical of colonial farms in Kenya.

At the roadside, my heart throbbed with anticipation of my first bus ride; I had never ridden in any motor vehicle before. I kept an eye down the road, eager to sit idle for all the 18 miles to Nakuru town.

Will the trip last the entire day? I asked myself. That would be such a thrill.

Before long, intermittent honks similar to sounds of harmonica alerted us before the bottom-blue and top-white bus came into view. The driver could have saved his energy. With no other cars, and on a dirt country road, no one could have missed the billowing dust that fouled the fresh, cool air we enjoyed since we left home.

When we boarded, the conductor directed us to vacant seats in the middle. My father (Baba) stood in the aisle so I could sit first. The bus started moving. He held onto two seat frames and told me to hurry. I scooted under his arm, sat on the edge of the seat, and swiveled Waweru to my front the way Mother and other village women did when they prepared to sit or carry loads on their backs. I then leaned back, my little brother's temple on my chest.

Baba sat behind me, his hat on, still clad in his employer's issued winter-like gray coat.

Two *makanga* (baggage and passenger handlers) sat in front. Whenever our bus stopped, they rushed off to unload or load the passengers' baggage in the overhead carrier and the compartment at the back.

A third man, who showed us to our seats, sat alone across from the makanga. He collected bus fare and gave change.

Any person who talked on that bus spoke in Gĩkũyũ.

Since we left home, Waweru slept or looked at me with sunken eyes, his body lethargic—too sick to cry or want food. I distracted myself by looking at trees zoom backward the faster the bus moved. The sight fascinated me, and soon the motion soothed and made me doze off and on.

We came to a fork, where a tarmac road emptied into two dirt roads—the one our bus drove on and another almost parallel to ours that looped northwards.

When the bus slowed, the conductor called out, "*Mailikumi! Mailikumi!*" (Ten Miles! Ten Miles!).

Baba leaned toward me and pointed.

"That road goes to Bahati Market," he said, "and all the way to Nyeri. This stage is ten miles from Nakuru town where the tarmac road goes."

The driver parked the bus on a well-beaten shoulder. We remained there for about five minutes while people got off and others boarded.

When the bus entered the wider, tarmacked road, the ride became smoother. I released my grip on the side of my seat.

Without our bus whipping dust to the skies as before, twice with the help of two cars when they drove by, I enjoyed a countryside free of dust-ridden trees and shrubs. I liked also that more vehicles zoomed by and, on tarmac, they did not blow any dust. I now sat upright and relished the greenery, with an occasional herd of cows or goats scattered on the rambling landscape.

Before we arrived in town, the bus entered a tarmacked and wider road where cars and lorries drove in one direction only. Passengers said it was Nakuru/Nairobi Road. Another road ran parallel to ours, farther on, where cars headed in the opposite direction.

Trees that I learned years later were jacarandas lined between the two roads. They looked as if somebody planted them. Well-trimmed grass carpeted the ground, and purple flowers sprouted on the crowns of the trees as if they were giant bouquets.

Nobody planted trees in Solai—at least not that I was aware of. But all kinds of indigenous trees like *mũrema* and *mũtamaiyũ* in different sizes and shapes, short grass, tall grass, shrubs, and creepers, and even wild fruits grew, and others intertwined just the way nature created them.

Did I prefer the jacarandas and managed landscape over the free-for-all Solai vegetation? Not really. It could not have occurred to me then to compare or consider that.

When our bus entered Nakuru, blooming bougainvillea appeared on the sides of the street. The town looked clean as if townspeople swept and washed it every day, unlike our dirt road and footpaths.

The bus drove along a roundabout and I hung onto the seat's frame so I wouldn't slide into the aisle.

I saw more cars and buses than I ever thought existed. Pedestrians hurried back and forth. Others walked so close to vehicles without concern that the drivers could run them over.

The terminal filled with parked buses, while *makangas* shouted their buses' destinations.

Ours shouted, "*Mwisho! Mwisho!*" (Last stop! Last stop!)

When the bus slowed toward its designated parking spot, the luggage handlers opened the door and hopped out before the driver parked.

From the bus station, Baba held my hand, the only time he held me, unless I count, which I'll ignore for now, the afternoon he did so to whip me when I was four.

He now helped me cross two streets and dropped my hand when we reached the curb by the roundabout where our bus passed by.

I stayed close behind him as we walked on the shoulder of the Nairobi/Nakuru road. We covered about half a mile before we turned into another jacaranda-lined street that took us to Nakuru General Hospital.

Even hospital people grew trees, hedges, flowers, and well-trimmed grass between the rectangular stone buildings with red or green-tiled rooftops.

Baba marched toward the waiting room as if he were going home.

*

I am unsure how long he, Waweru, and I waited, seated with others—mainly barefoot women hugging their sick children—on benches along the corridor, before a nurse came to get us.

She led us to a room where we found a white doctor. He asked questions in his language, a language I never heard before, which I soon learned was English.

How the doctor looked fascinated me more than the language he spoke. I watched him, maybe even gawked, wishing I could touch and feel his fragile, skinless hand. Would he feel Pain? I wondered.

That was my second time to see a white person. My first sighting was at my mother's job three years prior, but that was at least from 50 feet away.

The nurse translated what the doctor said to Baba in Gîkũyũ.

Besides saying *"Mtoto yangu [Mtoto wangu] mgonjwa"* (my child is sick), Baba did not seem to know what else to say.

The doctor opened each of Wawerũ's withered eyes and looked. He put a stethoscope on his chest and listened.

"What happened to your brother?" the nurse asked me.

"He's sick and doesn't want to eat," I said, "and he watches me with half-open eyes."

After the doctor finished his check-up, he talked to the nurse. The nurse turned to Baba.

"Doctor says your son is too sick to return home," she said. "But he's too young to stay in the hospital alone."

I listened, confused.

"What does he want me to do?" Baba asked.

"He has admitted both of your children."

How could that be? I'm not sick, *I thought.*

I turned my head and looked at my father to assess his reaction.

He turned toward me.

"The hospital will look after you and your brother," he said.

"Okay," I said.

The doctor finished writing his instructions and gave the papers to the nurse. She took Wawerũ from me and let his head rest on her shoulder.

"*Ndūkamake. Nĩ tūkorora ciana ciaku wega*," (Don't worry; we'll take care of your children well), the nurse told Baba.

"*Nĩ wega*," (Thank you) Baba replied and then faced me. "Look out for your brother. I'll return to check on you," he said before he turned and left.

"Follow me," the nurse said.

I quickened my steps to keep up with her along the corridor while my mind churned. I had experienced more than my share of life for a tiny nine-year-old girl.

Of all my parents' dreams for me, their first daughter, neither of them expected me at my age to pad on hospital hallways on a mission to act as a surrogate mother to my little brother.

But there I was!

Chapter 3
Beginning

My parents and their ancestors came from Nyeri under the shadows of the snow-capped Mt. Kenya. Before the ravages of climate change stripped snow from its peaks, the mountain stood with all its majesty to protect and enhance the people's lives, their animals, and crops.

Because of its temperate weather, my tribe, Agĩkũyũ, called Nyeri the land of milk and honey. The community enjoyed four seasons, the coldest one named *Muoria Nyoni* (the one that froze birds) because some of them froze right on trees where they perched.

Then the British descended on Kenya and conquered the various micro-nations, one by one, as mentioned before, from Mombasa on the Indian Ocean to Lake Victoria to the west.

The micro-nations resisted and fought back (Taita Taveta is reported to have taken eight years to conquer), but they were no match for the British because of:

- Their superior weaponry of gunpowder that their government had unleashed on humankind
- Assault on smaller, weaker nations
- Local collaborators and traitors who they recruited and raised to positions of prominence to help suppress the uprisings and later to oppress and contain the masses.

When the British crushed the inhabitants at the end of the 19th and early 20th centuries, they took two decades to demarcate, zone, and shape Kenya in the image of England. They turned it into a colony in 1920.

By then, the conquerors had relegated Agĩkũyũ people and other natives to the basement of society. Natives now tottered several notches below the Indians, and a hundredfold below the whites.

From then on, Africans got better treatment if they converted to Christianity and took their children to the few schools Missionaries built, not only for formal education but also to study Christianity.

But most people, like my father, became disoriented. Many of them had witnessed the mayhem of invasion, and now the invaders had thrown them into a new system that obliterated everything they knew and introduced them to a cash economy.

To operate in the new government, men left their families (to join them later or not at all) and homelands, now designated *native reserves*, and sought jobs in towns or on European farms.

*

On a farm managed by Kamunge, a British colonizer, in the Great Rift Valley, a little girl drew her first breath. My parents named her Wanjirũ, after Baba's mother. That fluke of nature thrust me into a first daughter's spot, which gave me an edge—ahead of future daughters but below the sons and, of course, eons below the British.

At the time, my family lived at *Kĩrĩma-inĩ* (by the mountain), a homestead nestled in the farthest west corner of the farm. Beyond the grassland, we had no neighbors for about two or three miles.

A quarter of a mile away, the land sloped to Tindaress River where Baba's goats drank and we drew our water.

Women in my family filled their five-gallon containers, tied them with leather straps, and hoisted them on their backs. They then inched back up the incline—like climbing a mountain—hence the name *Kĩrĩma-inĩ.*

If a carrier did not arch her back enough, which had happened at least once, the container rolled off her back to end up right down at the river, endangering her legs.

Lucky for me, a political turmoil broke out in Kenya and the farm owner ordered my family to move before I grew old enough to tackle that incline.

*

Our compound, a version of the Gĩkũyũ traditional circular homestead, with a courtyard at the center, contained five houses. Members of my family occupied the houses in singles, doubles, or triples.

Baba lived in *thingira* (man's house), set in a strategic spot with a view of the entire courtyard.

Nyũmba (house), the biggest among the five houses, belonged to my mother, which she shared with two of her youngest children before they moved to the boys' cottage. But when her two girls—my sister Tabitha and I—came along, nyũmba became our sleeping quarters, too.

My three brothers shared one cottage and the goats shared the other. Some of Baba's goats occupied the fifth house that Kaguyu, Baba's ex-wife, lived in before.

Our stick and mud-plastered circular houses had conical thatched roofs. A central supporting wood pillar extended for about a foot above the peak.

I read material by writers and others who distribute information about Africa referring to those types of houses as *huts*. To us, they were suitable and comfortable houses that retained heat during cold periods and coolness during the hot months. Besides, farmworkers like my parents lived and worked at the pleasure of their employer, who could have ordered a family or families to move or leave the farm at a moment's notice.

The houses contained no windows except for the three-to-four-inch gaps between the rafters and the walls that provided ventilation. Doors let in additional fresh air because we left them ajar until after dusk.

Our ventilation failed only if someone used wet firewood or before it turned bone-dry. Then smoke became excessive and stung our eyes. We blew and fanned it away from our faces. A cough or a sneeze, however, never trailed too far from us, especially when Mother agitated the fire with a piece of wood or fanned it so it could catch on and burn faster to dispel smoke.

The granary, the only structure free of mud, had walls woven from dry vines, and a grass-thatched peaked roof. It rested on stilts of at least two feet high to provide ventilation and keep any animals and insects out.

Mother used the granary to store the family's harvest from the plot allocated to Baba by the farm's owner. This included maize, beans, peas, potatoes, and the following year's seeds. The granary also held empty bags, tools, and various other items. Without refrigeration and nyũmba too warm, Mother also stored cooked food that the family ate over several days.

Next came the chicken coop, built of wood and chicken wire, and much smaller than the granary.

The structures all faced the courtyard, fenced with dry wood sticks and reinforced by shrubs and creepers planted on the exterior. These also closed holes caused by age deterioration or damage from Baba's he-goats when they head-butted each other, most times fighting for a female.

The gate, made of two posts on each side with rungs like a ladder, completed the compound. It stayed open from morning to evening.

Before dusk, after chickens and goats turned in for the night, Baba or my two older brothers slid several eight-foot-long pieces of wood across the entrance atop the rungs to prevent animals larger than a chicken or cat to weasel through at night.

My parents went to work early every morning for Kamunge, six days a week. Sunday was their day off when they attended to their chores or ran their businesses.

Mother sold snuff tobacco while Baba sold hides and skins straps to women who used them to strap loads of firewood or water containers they carried on their backs.

To sell their wares, my parents left before dawn on two Sundays each month. They walked seven miles to Kabazi Market on the other side of Jumatatu Mountain to the east on one Sunday. But on the Sunday after payday, they went to the bigger Bahati market ten miles away.

When my parents returned home, my mother cooked and did her other household chores. But Baba needed a break after the long day. He rested, drank his homemade beer, and admired his animals.

Chapter 4

My Earliest Memory

My life up to age four, or perhaps five, is dotted by brief moments of memories and blurs frozen in time. One of those foggy incidents is when I saw a strange woman on thingira's porch. Confused, I gawked at her. I failed to understand her status or significance in our family. I remained confused eve after I learned who she was.

Another incident was when in adulthood my brother Simon told me: "You were a stubborn child."

"Why do you say that?" I asked.

"If I let you, you'd have latched onto my back until you were four years or older."

It so happened Simon both babysat me and herded our father's goats. He carried me wherever he took the herd in the sprawling savanna.

During one incident around the time I saw the woman in our courtyard, he and I reached a clear footpath where he put me down. "You can walk now."

I balked and pursed my lips.

"Let's go," he said and took four steps forward.

Instead of following him, I slumped down cross-legged in the middle of the trail.

He walked on, rounded the bend, and disappeared.

About a minute later, my pout stiffer, I caught him peering from the tall wiregrass. He backed away twice before he realized I would not fall for his trick. He marched toward me, arguing with himself "about this child," and threw me on his back.

But my first concrete memory came about because we used the sprawl of the wooded area outside our compound as our toilet.

I can only speculate why my parents did not think to dig a toilet. Or they did not think we needed one amid all that vacant country.

To potty-train me, Mother led me outside the gate, walked along a footpath about ten to twenty yards from the homestead, pointed me to a spot inland, and stood to watch like a sentry. Training ceased when I turned four years old after the birth of my little brother, Gîthûi.

Mother had trained me well by then, but the vast wild thicket of trees, shrubs, and tall grass outside that spread for miles, it seemed, intimidated me. Left without support, I improvised.

Whenever the urge hit me, I looked this way and that before I sneaked to the farthest part of the fence behind nyûmba and deposited my little turds.

The first time Mother discovered a mound before the chickens cleared it, she scooped it with velvety *maigoya* leaves from the fencing shrubs.

"You're old enough to know better," she said, her index finger pointed at me. She promised dire consequences if it happened again.

I did not mean to defy my mother; I just wanted to get relief without fear. But now that she had interfered, I needed to come up with more secure hideouts where I could sneak undetected.

My sister Tabitha was two, too young to snitch on me. Joseph, two years older than me, preferred to join goat herders in the savanna or to romp farther than the courtyard.

A dash under the eaves behind nyũmba became my new strategy. To my dismay, the minute Mother reached her doorway, coming from the granary, she stopped, scrunched her face, and sniffed this way and that. She set down *gîtarũrũ* (the woven tray) she held and walked four steps toward one side of her house, stopped and sniffed, then turned and headed the other way.

"Has this child become dumber as she gets older?" Mother asked. "She has turned this homestead into her toilet."

How can she tell? I asked myself, surprised.

"Wanjirũ, come here!"

She stood by my pile, which now revolted me.

"Get *maigoya* and clean up your mess!"

I trotted to the fence and plucked leaves, one by one.

"That's enough," she said.

I hurried back, my little hands loaded, my face contorted, and my lips puckered. Unmotivated to do her bidding, I hung my head and kept up my sniffles.

"Go on. Scoop it."

I bent over, my sniffles louder. My shaky, poorly coordinated hands trembled.

Mother yanked the leaves from me just in the nick of time.

"If you poop anywhere around or inside this courtyard again," she warned, "you'll scoop it with your bare hands."

I looked up at my mother, wide-eyed, and whimpered.

With bare hands? She couldn't be serious.

Her warning worried me, but the wood expanse outside our compound worried me more. Even at four, going on five, I kept quiet rather than tell my mother the fear that shook my little heart and have her minimize or brush aside my concerns, claiming I was old enough.

So, my mother's reprimands and warnings failed to take hold. Whether I braved the grassy area in between is lost to memory. But I recall that whenever I felt the urge, I dashed to wherever I thought my secret safest.

Soon, I ran out of options on how to outwit my mother.

When the next opportunity rolled around, like a revelation, I realized, nyũmba, her maze-like house, would solve my dilemma. It covered about 700 square feet, partitioned into three rooms, two of them semi-dark.

Inside the threshold was a wall with two entrances. They both led to the living area that held the fire pit near the center pillar. We used the bigger right entrance most times because it let more light in and was closer to the small hallway that separated our mother's bedroom from the tiny room where my sister Tabitha and I shared a bed.

I entered through the larger entrance and skulked like a little stalker to ensure no one remained indoors. I then headed toward the sleeping area. Pitch dark, it was difficult for anyone unfamiliar with Mother's bedroom to navigate through. But she and I shared her bed until I turned two years old. I could, therefore, sense my way around even if I shut my eyes.

I left my package at the darkest corner, sure Mother would never find out.

I believed she possessed special powers that enabled her to find out things, but I doubted she could be that good. I returned to the courtyard and soon forgot my secret.

To my horror, when Mother entered her bedroom, her reaction reached the porch where, by then, my sister and I sat doing child stuff.

"The child has done it again! Wanjirũ!" Mother called out as she rushed back to the doorway.

I stood when she appeared, my now idle hands close to my mouth, aware she found out my hideaway.

"What did I tell you?"

I had forgotten what she told me. I stared at her, my lower lip curled, my scrunched face full of misery.

"I said you would scoop it with your bare hands."

I strung out a series of whimpers.

"Is this child getting dumber?" my mother asked, loud enough for anyone in the courtyard to hear.

Her boisterous complaints did the unthinkable. They alerted Baba, who liked to join fights even if they didn't concern him.

He came from puttering near his *thingira* and grabbed my right arm. He dragged me along while I trotted behind to keep up.

At the shrubbery by the fence, he broke off a couple of stout twigs and started whipping my buttocks. I dropped to the ground, crossed my legs, and rocked side to side as I screamed and screamed and screamed. My eyes followed the path of the lashes, which landed on my exposed thighs while the hem of my little dress flew in all directions, my arms caught in the fracas. He spared my head, perhaps because of my tender age.

I learned much later, however, that Mother had said her children's heads were no-beat zones because she did not want them to grow up demented. But from an assault that I witnessed five years later, and others I learned about, she had little say about the beatings her children endured.

But she tried to intervene in my case.

"Run! Run! Run!" she said from yards away.

I saw her hand gestures and heard her voice, but nothing registered. Why doesn't she help me? flashed through my mind.

"This is a stubborn child," Baba said, and shook his head. He tossed his weapon by the fence as he walked away.

In less than a minute, my screams ran out of fuel and I settled for whimpers. I then rose and shuffled to the fence farthest from the gate and leaned my bruised body.

How do I stop being stubborn? What does stubborn mean? I wondered.

While I willed my muscles' throbs to stop, I resolved to brave the woods. Better outrun the big ogre that ate naughty children that Mother had threatened us with than suffer such pain.

After I made my decision, my mind wandered to other things.

I figured it was a Sunday because Baba did not leave for work. How will I tell the other days? Shall I have special powers like my mother when I grow up?

Later, at about ten or twelve, during one of my mother's relaxed conversations with us children, I learned Baba called me stubborn because I did not run, perhaps as a sign of repentance or submission.

"You should have run when he let go of your arm," Mother said.

But it still intrigued me how she concluded I was the culprit right away, even though no one saw me sneak into her bedroom.

She could not have suspected my brother Joseph because at six, going on seven, and a goat-herder in training, the woods never intimidated him. My sister Tabitha, at two going on three, was still enjoying potty training.

Despite that incident, I turned out one of the few lucky children in my family. Except for a palm swat Mother threw at me in my early teens that I ducked just in time, Baba's whipping remained the only physical parental assault I suffered when growing up.

But I witnessed a handful of my brothers' severe beatings and heard of others, which traumatized me for life as if I suffered the abuse myself.

Chapter 5

Varied Freedoms

My siblings and I enjoyed playing around the courtyard, especially before dusk or during moonlight. Some Saturday or Sunday evenings, Baba sat on a three-legged stool on his porch, his hat on his folded knee, from where he watched. At such times, we refrained or toned down our play.

Sometimes, when I forgot myself and played with unbridled energy, I stopped when I noticed his presence. I then threw him a glance to check whether he had noticed me.

We harbored a visceral fear of Baba, passed down from his older children. They viewed him as a disgruntled superman or like a stern god whom one did not dare cross. Before age seven, however, I had not yet developed that fear; I just followed my brothers' cues.

I sensed from a young age that when goats romped in the courtyard and we played alongside them, Baba never complained or reprimanded us. He seemed peaceful while he watched his goats and children play.

Goats, unlike us, enjoyed special treatment without reprimand or concern of who watched them. Well, except for three poor souls imprisoned in a four-foot-high wooden enclosure in nyũmba. They lived in that enclosure day and night. I doubt the space was big enough for them to lie down without stepping or bumping into each other.

Not once did I see them go outdoors to bask in the sun or stretch their legs. If one did, it was to the slaughter spot.

Besides seeing them for a moment or two through the cracks, I noticed those captive goats from their grunts, munches, or bumps.

My mother fed them a variety of green cuttings, potato peels or vegetable remnants, and water. Their stench permeated every clump of dirt and everything else in nyũmba and even wafted into the courtyard to mix with the other goats and chickens' smells. It did not bother us. We got used to those smells like owners of dogs and other animals.

When I grew old enough to question things around me, I wondered why those goats never joined the rest of the herd in their cottage. Later in my pre-teen years, I learned colonial laws forbade Africans from raising billy or nanny goats.

Agĩkũyũ, however, had always segregated and fattened goats for slaughter on special occasions, like engagement parties, the birth of a child, sacrifice, and other special occasions. I never witnessed such events because life on the farm was not conducive to such ceremonial slaughters.

But according to Mother, when I was a toddler, Baba took my two older brothers—David at ten and Simon at eight—for a male-bonding bush camp event for three days. They lived on meat and soups from a goat they took with them.

Otherwise, ordinary goats that slept in their cottage enjoyed total freedom. Evenings before their bedtime and mornings before they left for pasture, they stretched, socialized, suckled their young, stole, and ate anything edible we left lying around the courtyard. They fought, bleated, or made love without concern for Baba's reprimand. Well, unless it came to a weekend when he craved meat—especially when he drank—and then cut a throat of an unlucky goat.

Chickens seemed the freest members of our household. Perhaps our two cats—one gray and the other spotted—could have disagreed. Unbeknownst to them, however, they were working animals. Long before my brothers grew old enough to acquire hunting skills, our two cats were already avid hunters. They let no rodent venture into or close to our courtyard.

Freedom, therefore, belonged to the chickens: no herding off to pasture, no reprimands or beatings, and no chores. They came and went as they pleased, rested under houses or fence shade in the courtyard, or roamed in the surrounding grassland until evening. They ate stray grains

or the maize grains that Mother fed them, wild fruit, or
defenseless insects and larvae.

While hens provided eggs, the roosters kept time.
Mother relied on their timekeeping service often, especially
on market days when she needed to wake earlier than usual.
The roosters' crows became a point of reference—whether
something happened before or after the first, second, or
third crow.

Besides, chickens never went astray like goats or waited
for anybody to fetch them. At dusk, they rushed home to
beat darkness as if a predator chased them. As a child, it
fascinated me to watch a mother hen spew a series of cackles
as she hurried back and forth, gathering her chicks.

After chickens piled in, the able-bodied perched on a
two-foot-high stick bed across the coop; they disliked
sleeping on the floor. But weak and mother hens had little
choice. They headed to safe corners to avoid poop from
overhead. A moment's commotion ensued while the
overhead chickens slipped before they settled themselves
and the chicks scrambled under their mothers' wings.

Soon the whole hen community fell quiet and snoozed.
But a chicken could wake up at a moment's notice when it
lost its footing or slept with one eye open.

As I understand it today, chickens suffer no insomnia
worries. And unlike humans, lack of enough sleep does not
cause them side effects.

Besides the freedom our chickens enjoyed, few of them
met an untimely death. For undisclosed reasons, Baba never
ate wildlife, which category, according to him, chickens fell

under. As the head of our household, he owned the chickens and no one could eat them—at least not openly—without his permission. So, the chickens made merry, bred, and multiplied.

"Warama has a lot of chickens," family and an occasional visitor said.

While my family looked at the abundance with greedy eyes, Baba watched and admired *mahiũ make* (his animal wealth). He never remembered, or it never occurred to him, to tell Mother to slaughter a chicken. She had to nudge him that his children missed the delicacy. Even then, he sometimes took days to respond; perhaps to prove he did not bow to a woman's wish.

But my three older brothers—Njerũ (David), thirteen; Ndurumo (Simon), eleven; and Machira (Joseph), seven— did not wait for the mind-power games between my parents to play out. When they got a chance to eat chicken, they did just that.

They picked a Saturday when David was out of school— taking a break from his five-day long walk and his bullies— and my parents at work. Somehow, my sister Tabitha and I failed to notice. Perhaps my brothers just navigated around us.

Joseph remained in the woods, minding the goats, while David and Simon returned home to carry out their heist.

In nyũmba, the two thieves kindled the fire and put a large pot of water on. While it heated, they hunted for a chicken without chicks; a breeder lived to old age. When they located a suitable victim, they cornered and grabbed the poor chicken. One of them strangled it with his bare hands.

Strangling animals went against our family's meat culture. A legitimate butcher, my parents said, cut the throat and held it steady until the last drop drained to avoid bloody meat. But my brothers could not gamble on accidental sputters.

The strangler dunked the chicken headfirst into the steaming water, leaving the legs stuck out for easy turning and handling.

When they estimated one side of the chicken cooked, they rolled it to the other.

Occasionally, one of them went outside to check whether the smell reached the courtyard or took a peek from the door in case an adult or one of my parents returned home.

When they determined the chicken cooked, David pulled it out by the legs and let the water drain without burning himself, and carried the feast to the woods.

While he and Joseph plucked the chicken over a bed of leafy branch cuttings, Simon cleaned to ensure nyũmba looked as they found it. He poured the hot water outside the gate where a rogue feather would not raise suspicion. He then washed the pot and scanned inside the house for any stray evidence.

Not once did anyone miss the devoured chickens.

My brothers waited until their late teens to tell us children and Mother the story, after their rites of passage to adulthood, when Baba's beatings ceased.

We showered them with admiration for their ingenuity.

"I should have devised a way to feed my children all those chickens," Mother quipped.

Nobody dared or cared to enlighten Baba, who remained in the dark then and forever.

Chapter 6

David

Too young to appreciate my three brothers' exploits, I watched with envy when they pranked and sprinted around the courtyard. I longed to join them. But Joseph, two years older than me, dismissed me offhand; he preferred to play with the boys, not with a little girl.

I knew Simon and Joseph herded goats. And David, the oldest, spent most of his days elsewhere, which I was not clear about where until three years later when I realized he spent his time in school. On weekends, he joined the other two to take goats to pasture.

From the boisterous activities my three brothers engaged in, one would think they had no worries. But the older they got, the more unpleasant incidents came their way beside Baba's violence toward them, which I had not known about yet either.

David seemed to have a monopoly on childhood traumas. He suffered his first bout after Simon's birth. Within a week, he quit eating, stopped thriving and, in time, regressed to a baby—a listless baby who could not talk, cry, or walk.

Mother massaged the little body with warm castor oil while Baba scavenged for medicinal herbs. Mother boiled those herbs and fed David sips of the liquid.

When my parents' endeavors failed, they consulted a medicine man and then another. The boy failed to respond. His body continued to shrivel. Mother gave up on him. But she force-fed him a few teaspoons of goat's milk or millet porridge while she waited for him to die.

"I wanted to satisfy myself that I had done everything I could to save my child," she said later.

After three months, to Mother's relief, David surprised her. In case it was a sign of worse things to come, she and Baba kept it to themselves for at least a week.

But, like a wilted plant in a desert after a rainfall, David emerged from his stupor. He started eating small amounts of food. After a month, he picked up where he left off and became a bouncy, handsome toddler.

The family dubbed it a mystery.

In later years when Mother talked about our childhood mishaps, she always included that "mysterious" illness.

I asked David about it in December 2017. He told me the story as if it were still a mystery. I resisted injecting my opinion that he may have suffered from severe abandonment when Mother's singular focus on him ceased and, instead, shifted to his newborn brother.

* * *

Mother took me with her to her job or the garden until I turned two, when she weaned me like the rest and turned me over to a babysitter. By then, David's *mysterious* illness had faded from the family's collective memory. She usually left him, Simon, and Joseph at home and asked one of our half-siblings from Baba's first family, who now lived behind our compound, to keep an eye on them.

One late afternoon, David and Simon played hide-and-seek around the courtyard while Joseph tagged along. They hid behind or under anything that could conceal them. After several rounds, they ran out of places to hide. When David's next turn came, he figured one place Simon could not suspect.

"Shut your eyes," David said to Simon.

He then rounded to the front, stepped on the granary's jutting boards, opened the small creaky door, and entered. He rummaged through a multitude of Mother's bags and other household items. Before he settled on a spot, a "beehive" distracted him.

Bees had colonized an empty four or five-gallon gourd with a wide opening where Mother stored grains like beans and black-eyed peas. The gourd lay sideways and guard bees rested on or buzzed around the opening.

"Can I open my eyes?" Simon asked. Silence. "Can I open now?"

David focused on his *lucky* find and did not want to talk and disturb the bees. They produced sweet honey similar to the kind Baba brought home when he harvested his beehives.

Excited, David longed to harvest honey like his father. He would surprise Simon and Joseph with honey, which seemed so grownup.

"You're taking too long," Simon said.

David remained quiet. He hesitated, unsure of what Baba used.

He climbed out of the granary and went in search of a harvesting tool.

He scavenged around the courtyard.

Simon opened his eyes when he heard David walk about.

"You don't want me to find you?"

"Just wait," David said. "I'll show you something."

At the fence, he broke the straightest stick he could find. Back in the granary, he took his position.

He pointed the stick to the gourd beehive's opening and progressed gently so as not to disturb the bees' activities. The stick bumped into a barrier. David twisted it and pulled it out. Its tip contained a dab of honey.

Before he dipped in the stick again for a better harvest, the bees mobilized.

The minute they cleared the opening, they buzzed and flew in all directions

David dropped the stick and willed his limbs to get him to the exit. He yelled and flailed his arms as he tripped on bags, tools, and other items.

The lead bees joined in the melee.

When he reached the door, he put one foot on the stepping board and half tumbled to the ground, a mob of bees right behind him.

Simon and Joseph scurried into the house and shut the door. The two grownups behind the homestead did the same.

The bees poured out and spread into the courtyard.

Confused, it didn't occur to David to follow his brothers. Instead, he hollered and ran toward the main entrance and took the footpath that led away from home.

With an obvious target, the bees flew in a trail formation and followed in full attack mode.

*

My half-brother Waigwa, in his early twenties, walked home from work. From a distance, he saw bees circling a spot. On getting closer, it looked like a small anthill. Closer still, he heard intermittent, faint whimpers underneath the bees and noticed streaks of clothing. He took off his coat and swatted the bees as fast as he could. He ducked in amidst the stingers and scooped David, threw the coat over his head, and rushed to safety.

When Mother arrived home, and before she learned what attacked David, she took one look at him and let out a piercing scream. Every inch of her son's body looked bloated. His swollen tongue stuck out, too big for his mouth. He had reduced his cries to grunts.

Mother plucked every sting from David's body before she and Baba started another round of home remedies. Besides the herbs, Mother washed David with Baba's homemade beer every day. After every wash, she gave him a sip or two.

Nobody expected David to survive that time. But once again, he surprised the family when death gave him another chance.

Forevermore, no matter what Waigwa did, Mother reserved a soft spot in her heart for him for saving her son.

Chapter 7

Simon

David did not hold a monopoly on childhood survival; other incidents came along and punctuated his rocky young life.

One such incident took place a year before the bees' attack when, one afternoon, Mother heard yells from the courtyard. She jumped into defense mode, only to realize the predator and victim were her own.

David, wide-eyed and mouth agape, froze where he stood.

Simon bent, his arms sagged at his side, while one of his eyes dangled down to his cheekbone. He screamed as if his injured eye preyed on him.

Mother rushed him inside her house. She examined him and, ever so carefully, repositioned the blob.

She soothed him.

"What happened?" she asked when he managed to speak.

"David poked me."

"It's not me. It's the thorn," David said from where he now stood by the door.

After things calmed somewhat, Mother questioned my two brothers. After she and Baba weighed the matter, they determined there was no animosity between the two. It was an accident; the boys were just playing, they said.

In about ten days, besides a slight sensitivity, Simon's eye seemed almost *normal*. He, like everyone else, was unaware he now had a disabled left eye.

The family resumed its regular rhythm and from then on, nobody paid attention to Simon's changing eye. By the time it settled in its permanent state, it showed an auburn color and a blue center that contrasted with the uninjured eye that remained deep dark navy-blue.

I noticed Simon's eye in my teens when Mother and another woman talked about the vagaries of raising children.

"Hard to keep an eye on them every waking moment," Mother said. "My oldest poked his brother's eye while I was right there at home."

Except for that one time, none of us siblings or our parents paid attention or mentioned Simon's eye.

In adulthood, I longed to ask how well he saw with that eye or his side of the story, but I never gathered enough courage. Others noticed, too, but said nothing in his presence.

When I mentioned him to my younger relatives who were unfamiliar with him, a voice always chimed in, "Is it the uncle with the eye?"

"Yes," I would say.

I learned the damage to Simon's eye decades later when I visited him at his home in June 2016. I noticed his eyes looked the same, the auburn/blue center gone. That gave me the courage to raise the subject.

"Did you do something to your eyes?" I asked. "They look so clear."

"I consulted an eye doctor last year," he said.

"You did?"

"Yes. He fixed it."

"Oh, that's great." It did not occur to me to ask what the eye doctor did.

"The doctor said if I went to the hospital when it happened, they would have saved my eye."

Simon said the last part with a tone full of regret. It touched me. I hesitated for a second or so before I gathered more courage and asked him another critical question.

"Does the eye see?"

"No," he said.

"Oh," I said and kept quiet.

Simon said children get into all sorts of accidents before they grow up. He rehashed the story of his childhood incident when he and David played with thorns and other homemade toys. When he finished, I wanted more answers, like:

When did he realize his eye could not see?

Did it bother him when he found out?

As an adult, did he feel resentment toward David?

Courage failed me. Besides, I did not want to plant a negative seed about something that I believed, perhaps hoped, never bothered Simon.

Meanwhile, he changed the subject and embarked on a donkey story I had heard about as a young girl.

*

Before I was born, Baba owned three donkeys, one of them named Toto and the other Njeremani. While the children played in the courtyard, David rushed Toto the way I later saw my brothers dash toward a goat in the name of fun. Not interested in David's kind of fun, Toto kicked him to the ground. Then turned around and raised its right hoof to finish what it started.

Amidst his hollers, and startled by Toto's behavior, David opened his mouth wide.

Toto's hoof landed on his cheek. Satisfied, the animal raised his leg and sauntered away.

Mother ran outdoors to save her child yet again.

When she later put water in David's mouth to wash the blood off, and to assess the damage, the water poured right through the cheek. After David went through another healing regimen, he remained with a half-moon scar on his cheek that he still carries today.

Poor Toto was prone to anger. When he got angry, he snapped his kick and then walked away. But for whatever reason, he carried it too far that time for his wellbeing. Baba beat him with sticks until he got tired. He then disowned Toto. The animal took a while to recuperate before anyone agreed to buy him.

Those childhood traumas of abandonment *mystery*, the bees, and the donkey attack took place before David started school and before Aunt Julia, my father's baby sister, stepped in and threw her weight around, which, although well-intentioned, brought David another slew of childhood hardships.

Chapter 8
The Dare

Aunt Julia visited my family when I was a year old. She soon became disappointed when she learned David had not started school. When she spoke to Baba about it, he said he wanted the nine-year-old to get older.

According to him, David was not old or strong enough to tackle a five or six-mile walk over Jumatatu Mountain range to the one-room school at Ndege's farm.

Aunt Julia did not care for excuses. She threw a fuss that David needed to attend school without further delay. Unlike my parents, Aunt Julia had gone to school and was financially better off than they were. They, therefore, respected her and went along with about anything she suggested.

She had intervened a year earlier when she visited and took Gĩthũi-big, the last son of Baba's first family. He now attended school in Mũrang'a where he lived with Aunt Julia's boyfriend's family.

At the end of her visit, she took David as well, and the two traveled to Nyeri, about 80 miles away.

She enrolled him in a school close to Nyeri General Hospital, where she worked as a nurse. In a year, without goat-herding and with a better diet, David thrived into a healthy, vibrant boy.

But his life was about to change. His living with Aunt Julia in a single room interfered with her personal and work schedule. She also decided he needed company because he arrived home from school before she got off work.

She, already married and divorced, had established her home five years earlier when she bought a five-acre piece of land in Irūri, Gataka-inî, and built an L-shaped house.

Njerū-big, Baba's first son, lived there with his wife, Njoki, and their three-year-old son, Mwangi. They minded the land and livestock and kept Aunt Julia's home maintained. She stayed in the house when she took her annual leave or visited on her off days.

When she considered her living arrangement, she decided a change would not only improve her social life, but would also give David a family life.

She took him to her home, registered him at Kanyota Primary School, and left him in care of Njerū-big and his wife Njoki.

Months later, back in Solai, Baba heard of an outbreak of hunger in Nyeri known as *Ng'aragu ya Gathūa*. But my parents believed David lived with Aunt Julia. And because she did not live off her land where a dry spell could devastate her livelihood, they did not fret about their son's wellbeing.

But on his way home one day, Baba met a man who had recently visited Nyeri. The man told Baba how hunger had devastated the whole of Nyeri.

"When I saw your boy," the man said, "I failed to understand why you let him remain there."

"He looked that bad?"

"Only an orphan would look like that."

"Are you sure it was my boy?"

"Of course it was your boy," the man said. "I stopped by your sister's, but she wasn't there."

Back home, Baba and Mother doubted the man's story. But within three months, Baba received a letter in which Aunt Julia confirmed David now lived with Njerũ-big's family.

*

Njerũ-big, the first son of the family, named after Baba's father, never got along with his father. Friction between the two may have started when he resisted Baba's cruelty and poor treatment or fought back.

The father and son relationship reached a breaking point one Sunday afternoon in 1945 when Baba and Kaguyu (Njerũ-big's mother) threw a small drinking party for a handful of close friends. By late afternoon, guests had left except for two men.

The four kept the party going. But it took a different turn when Baba and Kaguyu got into a fight. The two guests eased out of the house and waited in the courtyard to give the couple space to settle their differences.

From his house at the back of the homestead, Njerũ-big shot out when he heard a scuffle and his mother's loud torrent of complaints. He rummaged for a good-size stick at the periphery of the courtyard.

Stick in hand, he marched toward his mother's house to teach his father a lesson.

To his frustration, the two men at the courtyard grabbed and restrained him.

"There won't be any more fighting today," one man said.

To cool his fury, Njerũ-big turned and rounded to the back of the homestead where young maize plants grew. He swung the stick with all the energy he could muster and cleared half the garden as a scythe would.

The following morning, he left Kîrîma-inî in a huff and swore never to return to Solai.

And now, Aunt Julia, without checking with Baba, appointed the same Njerũ-big and his lazy wife as the guardians of Njerũ-little aka David, born of a wife who had allegedly edged his mother out of the limelight in the Warama household, sentiments that his sister Gathoni shared with me decades later.

*

Back then, Baba did not reply to Aunt Julia's letter.

Instead, he took a Saturday off and traveled to Nyeri—an entire day's safari in those days. When he knocked on Njerũ-big's door, he and his wife were so surprised they thought somebody died.

Baba had not returned to Nyeri since twenty years prior when he whisked his family out and turned his back on Gĩkũyũland.

"No, everyone is okay in Solai," Baba said. "But I heard things have become difficult. That people are dying of hunger."

"We are getting by."

After supper of sweet potatoes, a third of a normal portion, Njoki prepared a plank bed in the wooden cottage next to Aunt Julia's house. Baba, David, and little Mwangi slept in the cottage.

When all went quiet, Baba dug in his bag and produced a whole cooked fatty goat's head. He unwrapped it and with his pocket knife carved slices of meat. He and the boys ate to their fill and Baba returned the clean skull to his bag to discard later.

"Njeru, Njeru, wake up," Baba shook David at dawn.

"Aaah..."

"Get up. We are going home."

"Our home?"

Before Baba confirmed, David had shot up and scrambled for his clothes.

He remained in the courtyard while Baba knocked at the big house.

"I'm taking Njerũ-little with me," Baba said when Njerũ-big came to the door.

"I thought you would stay for a few days."

"No. I need to get back to work."

"You don't have to take him. We are getting by okay."

"I think it'll be easier for your family without him."

*

When Baba and his now almost-eleven-year-old son neared Kĩrĩma-inĩ and David recognized our homestead, he quickened his shuffle, rounded the fence, and reached the entrance ahead of Baba. Mother, seated at her porch shelling beans, stopped to observe the little boy in well-worn shorts and a little jacket. He swayed side-to-side as if every step he took tortured him. But the boy seemed in high spirits.

What a strange child! Mother thought.

Meanwhile, Baba appeared at the entrance.

In a second, Mother shrieked. She dumped the tray; half the beans scattered to the ground while she rushed to meet her son.

"Oh! *Mwana wakwa!*" (Oh! My child!) Mother said. "*Nĩmanyonjeria mwana!*" They have maimed my child!

Surprised by Mother's reaction, David froze.

When she reached him, she inspected him from head to foot. Meanwhile, she talked to herself as only a mother could without seeming nutty.

Various sizes of jigger clusters littered his feet—between his toes, on toe-tips, and under toenails, heels, and on the sides. His soles were the only parts of his feet that remained uninfected. His hands and even his elbows displayed a scatter of little bumps.

In the following days, Mother used a safety pin to dig out and remove the jiggers. She started with the fattest little white balls that she removed in stages so as not to leave too many gaping wounds. She then washed the sores with Dettol amid David's winces.

In about a week, she cleared flea larvae from his body. While his sores healed, she fed him as if she were caring for an invalid.

As Baba did when Mother gave birth, he slaughtered a goat so David could feed on soups. It took him more than a month to recover from a year's neglect and starvation.

I never heard whether Aunt Julia saw David in that state, and if she did—shame on her. But when she learned Baba took David back to Solai, she wrote him a scathing letter and accused him of preferring his children to remain illiterate.

"Now that you have withdrawn Njerũ-little from school," she accused. "We'll see whether you can afford to educate him."

Baba did not reply to his sister's letter or address the subject again. But deep inside him, I do not doubt it was game on.

My family repeated the story of that dare so many times that every member of the family alive heard about it, or, if unborn, heard it when they arrived.

Chapter 9
Dare's Challenges

According to my half-brother Waigwa, when he read Aunt Julia's letter to Baba, he scoffed and made slow nods when he heard:

"We'll see whether you can afford to educate Njeru-little."

After Waigwa finished reading, Baba took the letter and tucked it in his shirt pocket without comment. But the dare had hit home. *How dare she?* he may have asked himself.

From then on, David became a tool with which to prove a point between Baba and his sister, with education a mere byproduct.

He would get an education or remain illiterate, depending on who won the dare. I doubt it occurred to either wagerer to consider the effect of those two extreme life-defining options.

*

After David regained his health, at eleven years old, Baba made his move. He got time off from his job and marched to the one-room school at Ndege's farm. He talked to the headmaster, who agreed David could join grade two. To Baba, five or six miles over Jumatatu Mountain range or not, David would attend school.

David walked to school alone because the only other schoolboy in our area lived about three miles opposite our home.

Mother worried about the long distance. But, determined that her son get an education, she kept the worry to herself. She ensured he awoke early, got ready and drank his porridge, and carried the lunch she packed for him in a small kîondo. David soon accepted the distance as part of his life. But he worried about the horde of boys who ambushed and bullied him on his way home.

After he cleared Jumatatu Mountain incline, he found goatboys with their herds grazing nearby. The boys soon made contact. They touted, jeered, and called him a softie. In time, whenever the softie's and the toughs' paths crossed, the leader of the pack told David they would let him pass only if he won a boxing match with the youngest boy in the group.

The first time it happened, David eyed his opponent with satisfaction. The boy's small stature posed minimal threat.

The boys made a circle; the two boxers proceeded to the center, and it was game on.

"Begin," the leader said as he flapped his hand.

Amid a racket of roars and hoots, David knocked the boy down.

"That's not a fair match," the spectators protested.

The referee calmed them and settled the matter. David needed to beat the boy closest to his age, the second youngest, the referee said, and so it went.

When the match ended, perhaps in a tie, because the boxers got too exhausted to throw more punches, the referee declared David the winner, and presented him with a third boy.

David could handle two boys because they were younger or weaker than him, but he never got to the third one before the group roughed him up, kicked, and sent him home raggedy with scrapes and a bloody nose, which he wiped off before he arrived.

David caught a break for days when the boys herded goats in another part of the savanna. Or, if he saw them first, he ducked behind a bush and waited until their herds wandered inland. But the goatboys knew when he walked home, so they hung around longer.

He took part in three more impromptu *matches* before the mere sight or voices of his tormentors made him tremble and break into a sprint.

But he still suffered taunts and a kick or two from a determined boy.

David thought of dropping out of school. But that would create a bigger problem at home. Instead, he decided to evade the rascals altogether.

Whenever he heard their voices or saw goats grazing nearby, he ducked and hid in the nearby woods until the boys left. Or he crept through the thicket like a hunter and emerged ahead of where his tormentors camped.

As David grew older and wiser, he perfected his avoidance skills. He knew to scan the savanna for any herds of goats before he descended Jumatatu Mountain.

Now an emerging teen and a goat-herder on weekends, he already understood that sometimes a person needed more than fists or quick feet or even reason to settle a quarrel. He pondered on ways to defend himself before he settled on a weapon.

It took him an entire week to sculpt a one-and-a-half-foot-long club, with the smooth knobby end the size of a small orange. He hid his club half a mile before he arrived at school and retrieved it on his way home.

Just like before, whenever he spotted the goatboys, he dashed into the woods. But instead of sitting idle while he waited for their departure, he practiced his club swings. When he perfected the swings enough to stand up to any bully, he alerted his enemies that he had back-up.

He called out names of our family members from the top of Jumatatu Mountain, overlooking Kamunge's farm. His calls echoed for miles. Simon heard the calls and replied from wherever he herded goats. Even Mother heard David's calls when she came from her job or our garden.

I once heard a series of echoes and answers when I accompanied Mother to her job.

"Those are your brothers making all that racket," Mother told me.

It's anyone's guess whether the goatboys suspected David carried a weapon because they never waited to confront him again.

He hated that despite perfecting his swings, he never had a chance to crack his club on a boy's head or shoulders or even a back. With limited life experience, he failed to understand that in harsh rural areas, no skill went to waste.

Chapter 10

Snake and Boy

Besides goatherders, snakes were another part of our landscape. No child grew on the farm without encountering a snake.

One afternoon, on his way from school, David walked through the savanna. He swung his weapon now and then, unsure whether he would ever use it. He came by a snake coiled on the side of the footpath. When the snake saw him, it dashed inside the grassy area.

Snakes, like humans, relax and return to their activities as soon as the danger passes. But David, the danger, turned into a bully and denied the snake that right. He veered off the path and followed the snake where it sought refuge.

The minute the snake saw David, it took fright.

Boy and snake turned into the hunter and the hunted.

The snake slithered on grass and around scrubs, and David followed. They both gave their best, but David remained a step behind.

In a split second, the snake hissed, swung around with half its body off the ground, head cocked like a cobra. It had cowered enough.

David turned and begged his feet to carry him to safety.

When he covered enough distance, he glanced behind.

The snake slithered just feet away.

David weaved this way and that. But whenever he looked back, the chase remained on.

Panic set in.

Soon an idea came to him to slow down the snake.

He left the grassy area and ran along the rugged dirt narrow footpath.

The snake improvised. It glided from one grassy side of the path to the other.

The strange thing was, the snake knew to glide longer on grass—where it had an advantage.

The chase continued.

Exhausted, and out of options, David feared his heart could give up and he drop to the ground.

Fear gripped him when he thought of the possibility of the snake winning.

How does one defend himself against a possessed, crawling creature? he asked himself.

In a split second, he fell into a zone where his body, mind, and energy from another dimension aligned.

He swung around, his bare feet off the ground, his club in the air and down in one swoop.

It landed on the ideal target without a second to spare.

David's feet touched the ground less than two feet from where his club fell.

The four-foot snake's head lay smashed flat on the ground.

Its body flapped this way and that. It then made a series of crooked S's before it slowed and stopped altogether when life slithered away.

*

My family told such stories of childhood traumas in bits and pieces, but I never heard them from David. I asked him about his childhood in December 2014. He acted as enthusiastic in telling as I was in asking and listening. He even wrote points on a piece of paper so he did not miss any of them.

He termed some stories "mysterious."

Regarding the snake, he shook his head and marveled at the miraculous way he reacted all those decades ago.

"A phenomenon," he said, "divine intervention. Wait till I tell you the next story."

Chapter 11

Troughs

My parents would have worried, especially Mother, if they learned of the hazards David faced and endured as well as the likelihood of Baba losing the dare to his sister.

But David chose not to report the boys who terrorized him; he did not know where they lived. And, even if he did, he would have kept his mishaps to himself as children did in those days.

As for David's encounter with the snake, perhaps Baba would have said, "That'll show you not to fool around with wildlife."

Knowing my father, I'm convinced he would have reacted the same way about the trough phenomenon.

*

Kamunge's cows drank from concrete troughs scattered in the rambling cow pens and grazing fields. The regular troughs measured about ten-by-five feet and three feet high, with a seven-inch wall thickness where people could sit on top and splash water with their feet. But it was against farm rules for anyone to touch that water. Occasionally, however, boys sneaked in not only to splash water but also to enjoy a swim.

While David walked through the savanna one afternoon, he took a detour off the footpath to break the monotony. He came upon a trough tucked in a grassy, shrubby area with a sizeable tree growing close by. He had never seen such a big trough before. With a slight breeze and the blistering tropical sun, the water rippled and shimmered.

The sight enticed David, but, living in secluded Kîrîma-inî, he and Simon had not had a chance to collaborate with other boys and devise a way to construct a swimming pool and learn how to swim.

As my siblings and I learned later, when we moved to the village, boys had constructed two makeshift dams at Tindaress River where they swam without their parents' knowledge. They practiced despite the danger of drowning, and some even swallowed gobs of water while the rest cheered. According to my brother Joseph, who joined the swimming group, a couple of boys almost drowned before they got the hang of it.

Now, David stared at the inviting water and hated his lack of swimming skills. He soon realized, away from grownup's prying eyes, he could dip in, splash the water, and cool down. If he got overwhelmed, he figured, he would stand in the shallow trough. He could even drop by several times a week and learn how to swim by himself.

No one needed to know.

Decision made, he set down his school bag at a safe distance so his books would not get wet. He undressed, laid his uniform next to the bag, and crouched as he crept in case of an adult's wandering eyes afield.

He held onto the trough top to heave himself up, sit for a while and splash the water before he dipped in.

But not yet because he sensed a presence, and a flicker across the trough caught his eye.

A man's head appeared from behind the nearby tree. David dropped to his haunches and hoped the man had not seen him.

He waited. When he heard no rustles, he raised his head and kept his eyes level with the trough's surface.

The head had disappeared.

David stilled himself for another minute.

Then he rose cautiously, determined to get on with his swim.

The head reappeared in slow motion and revealed a white shirt. The man's unblinking eyes gazed at David, face stoic.

He ducked again.

Frustrated and apprehensive, it seemed odd that the man did not confront and reprimand him and that David did not sense any danger.

Because he was breaking farm rules, however, David figured it was just another grownup meddler, albeit a laid-back, considerate one.

It occurred to him to outwit the stranger.

He scooted and crept a few feet to the trough's narrow side and waited for a while.

He then emerged from his hideaway with a plan to rush and jump into the trough. But he failed to suppress his curiosity.

"I will take a quick peek at the tree," he told himself, "to ensure the man is gone."

Just as well. Now, the man's head and full chest slithered from behind the tree trunk. He turned his head sideways and bore his unblinking, pleading eyes on David. The sight rattled and terrified David.

David crouched and waited a minute. Without another glance, he dashed to where he left his clothes and schoolbag. He grabbed them and ran naked for a short distance before he stopped and dressed and hurried all the way home.

The following January, David suffered the wrath of the equatorial earth-scorching sun. He remembered his aborted swim the previous year and set toward the trough, determined to dip in once or twice, and rush out before any adult saw him.

He found the trough empty, the water all dried up. He held onto the top of the wall and peered down.

A puddle, like a tiny mirror reflection, shimmered way down at the bottom. David squinted and looked again.

I think I made a mistake. This is not it.

He backed off a couple of yards. Then let his eyes scan over the savanna landscape. The tree close by had lost most of its leaves, but its trunk brought back memories.

It was the right trough, all right.

He approached again and peered down one more time. Burdened by what he had *discovered*, and his narrow escape the previous time, he hustled out of there.

That evening, the secret gnawed at David. He needed to share it with someone to get relief. But how?

After supper, when the family sat around the hearth, he blurted out. "A boy said there is a giant trough on this farm."

"That's true," Mother said.

"Pupils thought he was lying."

"No."

"He said it goes deep into the ground?"

"Yes, it's a bottomless pit. Cows used to disappear before herdsmen realized what was going on," Mother said. "Kamunge had a trough built around it."

"Where is it?"

"That's not something to concern yourself with."

David never wandered off to that part of the savanna again.

*

During those lonely years, David grew tired of his tedious walk and the hassle in his life. One Friday morning, just before he started on Jumatatu Mountain incline, an idea struck him to take a day off and enjoy a long weekend.

That settled, he branched into the woods and spent the day terrorizing birds and squirrels by target-shooting them with gravel. Without a schedule, he ate his lunch earlier than usual. But not to worry, there were plenty of snacks available.

In the afternoon, he picked wild fruits and berries. He even squeezed in a nap before he headed home with a tired after-school look.

Because parents never visited their children's schools in those days, David figured Baba and Mother would remain in the dark. He could attend school whenever he chose or spend his days in the woods.

It never occurred to him to consider the school's reaction.

As the headmaster, and the only teacher, Mr. Jacob Rũrĩrĩ taught grades one to four. And he did not put up with slackers.

The following day, Saturday, he trekked the five miles to Kĩrĩma-inĩ to check on David.

David received two whippings—one at home and the other one when he reported to school that Monday.

With that kind of dedication, my parents spoke of Mr. Rũrĩrĩ with similar admiration given to modern-day celebrities.

As for David, he remained with no other option but to concentrate on his studies.

Chapter 12
Steamed Maize

I overlooked to mention that I came along after five boys, two dead and three alive, and my sister Tabitha came two years later. That gave Mother satisfaction because, in several years, her two daughters would ease her burden of female duties.

Mother started training me about a month before I turned six, starting with a trip to our garden. I felt special when she singled me out for the important mission. Before then, besides someone carrying me on his or her back, I doubt I had walked over 20 yards outside our homestead.

At our garden, Mother weeded and plucked green vegetables. Before she finished packing them, she stood, one hand on her hip, looked around the swath of greenery, and shook her head.

"This maize should be ready," she said.

I looked up at her, wondering what she meant.

"It's big," I said and raised my arm to touch one ear of maize. But I could not reach it.

"Yes, it's taller than you," Mother said. "But it's not ready for us to eat."

Before we left, she took the smaller *kîondo* that she stuffed with vegetables and put it in the big empty one. She then covered the load with an empty sack and hoisted it onto her back.

On our way home, we walked on a foot-and-tractor trail that ran alongside a green maize plantation that went on for acres and acres. When we reached halfway, Mother turned to the towering plants, yards away.

"This maize is ready," she said.

Then why did she say ours was not ready? I asked myself.

After another short distance, Mother stopped so suddenly I almost bumped into her from behind.

She gazed at the maize plants again and paused.

"My children should be eating maize this time of year," she said.

I stood and watched her, unsure what to make of it.

She glanced front and back, and around the savanna, and dashed into the plantation.

"Come," she called out to me.

I followed.

I found it hard to keep up with her. I tripped on tall, half-bent weeds. One time I fell but got up fast.

Deeper inside and with less sunlight, the weeds thinned and did not bother me anymore. I now dealt with the maize plants alone. I stooped or ducked or shut my eyes and swiped the hairy leaves off my face, neck, and arms. My exposed body parts itched.

Mother waited when she lost sight of me.

"Are you still coming?"

When she saw me, she continued.

She occasionally turned behind her and asked me, "Are you all right?"

Too focused on ducking the leaves, sometimes I forgot to answer her. She walked mere steps ahead, where I could see parts of her dress, and yet she seemed so far.

I caught up with her when we reached deep inside the bowels of the plantation where only slits of sunlight got through. I smelled the freshest air ever, but my skin felt uncomfortable, as if I were in an air-conditioned room.

Besides the thriving maize, the other plants had given up on life. Only scanty skinny weeds grew. The soil looked dark and damp—rich, adults would say.

Mother stopped and set her load down and separated the two bags. She put the vegetable kîondo on the ground next to me. "Wait here," she said before she slung the empty big kîondo's strap around her neck. It collapsed next to her left hip.

She went on the offensive, grabbed a maize ear, felt it with her hand, and left it alone or yanked it off and stuck it tip first into the kîondo. She then patted the plant's leaves back in place. She pulled ears at intervals, hurrying from one row to the next, sometimes skipping a row or two.

Why can't she pull them all in a row? I wondered when she disappeared.

I sensed she had enough when she reappeared with a bulging kîondo, set it down, and rearranged the maize ears.

"I'll be back," she said before she dashed into the maize plants. She reappeared with ears clutched in her arms.

After another disappearing act and back, she had enough maize.

She stacked the ears snugly in the kîondo, covered it with the empty sack and tucked it in. Then she hoisted her load onto her back and placed the smaller kîondo on top.

"Let's go," she said.

We sneaked out of the plantation ahead of where we entered.

After another stealthy glance up and down the trail and over the open savanna, Mother emerged into the open, turned toward home as if the detour never happened.

I trotted right behind her.

When we arrived home, Mother left the maize unloaded. She put the greens in an enamel basin and busied herself with her evening chores.

At dusk, when the household settled down to wait for supper and Baba drank his mug of tea, she tackled her load.

She husked the maize ears but left some husks on. She then arranged the now thinly husked ears in a big pot and poured in about a quart of water. To ensure no steam evaporated, she covered the ears with the loose husks and covered the pot with an iron lid.

When the maize cooked and Mother served us, my siblings and I filled the house with chatter, excited to eat the juicy, sweet first maize of the season.

"Shhh," she said and snapped her chin toward thingira.
We lowered our voices. I turned toward my brothers.
They wore questioning looks on their faces.

But for me, the matter became clear.

Since we left our garden and made the detour, I had not
put thought into Mother's actions. But in seconds, I now
connected her reaction to our noise with her behavior at the
maize plantation. I then understood Mother took maize
from someone else's garden and we should not let Baba
know.

She confirmed this when she did not include maize in
Baba's supper.

Today, I wonder what would have happened if Kamunge's
lookouts caught my mother in the act and told on her. I
presume Kamunge would have taken her to the police
station, followed by a fine and a criminal record. He had
done this to others, even children who sometimes stole
oranges from his orchard.

In addition, Kamunge would have rebuked Baba that he
had lost control of his wife, a rebuke British farmers threw
at African men to belittle or to show them how powerless
they were, even in their own homes.

(It has always been important to an African man,
especially during colonization, that if he could not control
anything else, he could at least manage his homestead.)

Kamunge would have also deducted his estimate of the
value of the maize from Baba's wages, which would have
earned Mother a generous whip lashing at home.

If only Baba caught her, perhaps Mother would have gotten away with just a whip treatment.

Mother's secret remained safe with me. I did not share it with a soul, not even my siblings. Somehow, I understood children did not cross or tell on their parents.

Even in adulthood, when we disclosed our childhood secrets, I kept my lips zipped. I did not want to embarrass Mother, especially because, as my siblings and I grew older, she was as strict as my father that we not take anything that belonged to someone else.

Based on the unrestrained way women in the village we moved to talked about female issues in my presence before I reached age eight, I now believe Mother thought I was too young to catch onto her maize theft.

As regards why our maize was not ready, it took me several years to realize Kamunge got his large tracts of plantation plowed and planted with maize and wheat first. Afterward, he sent his tractor to plow each of the 50 x 300-foot plots he temporarily allocated to married male employees. He then gave women laborers time off to prepare and plant their gardens.

But it took me more years before I learned why Kamunge plowed employees' plots, and it was not because he wanted to help or cared.

Chapter 13

My First Job

Two months after the maize incident, I woke up and found two women in our house. Because one woman remained in Mother's bedroom, I figured she overslept. The other woman cooked our porridge and Baba's tea that morning. When we finished, she insisted we children play outside.

"Is it my brother Macharia who has come?" Baba asked from the courtyard when he heard the baby's cries.

Mother, exhausted from the ordeal, needed to catch her breath. The women may not have known the answer, and they needed to prep the baby. So, no sound came from Mother's bedroom for about ten seconds.

"Yes," the two women then answered in unison, surprised, Mother said later, that Baba had correctly guessed the gender of the baby.

With that one question and answer, the baby's name became Macharia (or Morry, the name the family would later adopt).

Mother said nothing afterward. She could not be sure whether Baba mixed up the names, or he did it intentionally. But whatever the case, she could do nothing to undo the naming or fuss about her newborn's name. Besides, Agĩkũyũ did not rename children.

According to our custom—that is still upheld to this day—parents alternate naming their children between husband's and wife's families.

In my family's case, my parents named Gĩthũi, my two-year-old brother, after Baba's brother. But for my father's interference, they should have named Morry, the next boy, after Mother's brother.

I saw the baby when Mother left her bedroom holding him the following day, his head and part of his tiny hands uncovered by the towel wrapped around him. He smelled fresh and looked fragile with no skin and with jet-black slimy hair. I glanced at him as if he were an alien in our midst. My curiosity wore off as his body developed skin like ours, and Mother trimmed his slippery *womb hair*, as she called it.

My maternal grandmother, Nyandia, whom my younger sister Nyandia (Tabitha) is named after, came to see the baby. Grandmother wore a skirt with tiny prints under a brown dress, clipped together with safety pins at the shoulder and from the right armpit to the knee. Her earlobes dangled, but she wore no earrings.

It was the first and last time for me to see my grandmother.

Before she left the following day, I overheard her tell Mother that she and her husband, Ndurumo, would move to Nyeri. She said she wanted to remain behind, but he was in favor of going, thinking the turmoil in the country would get worse for those left on European farms.

A year later, I learned they joined the Gĩkũyũ exodus that the colonial government mobilized throughout the country.

*

Three weeks after my grandmother left, Mother had to return to work because it was the beginning of November, the height of the coffee cherry-picking season. The farm owner required everybody to report for work, and it was also the one period of the year that people earned more money than usual.

With a one-month-old baby, too young for Mother to strap on her back, she needed a babysitter. But she had few options.

David, the oldest, attended school the entire day. The second son, Simon, herded goats in the mornings and left to attend grade one in the afternoons. He left his eight-year-old brother, Joseph, to mind the goats by himself.

As the next in line, at six years old, Mother gave me the babysitting job, a job I got stuck with as if it were my childhood career.

Mother and I walked the three miles to the coffee plantation where she and others were scheduled to report for work. Because Morry's belly button could get sore, Mother carried him sideways across her chest in a sheet of cloth that she draped and tied over her shoulders like a sling.

When we arrived, I marveled at the sight of rows and rows of young coffee bushes; the highest stood about six feet tall. Their branches filled with clusters of red coffee cherries. Back then, I had not developed a concept of *beauty* or seen fruit trees. Otherwise, the plantation looked like a bounty vineyard with bushes bursting with red grapes before harvest.

Mother got a fresh sheet of cloth from her kîondo and spread it under a shady coffee bush. She laid Morry down and told me to sit and watch him. Whenever she progressed and lost sight of us, she moved us to a bush closer to her.

She took breaks several times to suckle Morry.

At lunchtime, she and I ate *gîtheri*, a mixture of maize, beans, potatoes, and vegetables, and drank water from a gourd.

"It's better to use a gourd," she said. "It keeps water cool longer than a bottle."

I said little unless Mother asked me a question, but she still talked as if she and I were having a conversation.

Many times, my eyes heavy with sleep, I nodded this and that, or sleep weighed on me and I dropped beside Morry and slept.

"Oh, the lookout slept," Mother said when she came to move us and I stirred and opened my eyes.

Morry's belly button healed when he was still light enough for me to carry on my back. I carried him in a ngoi, the traditional Gîkũyũ baby carrier, with the strap across my head. To prevent him from tumbling down, if my head jerked backward, Mother reinforced the ngoi with a sheet of cloth knotted across my chest.

Traditionally, Agĩkũyũ made ngoi from cured leather. But by the time I carried Morry in the 1950s, Mother used store-bought ngoi made from dark-green canvas. At the village we later moved to, she bought tailor-made ngoi from heavy khaki material. She dubbed it modern and as durable as canvas.

In time, like the traditional homesteads with courtyards, ngoi disappeared. If someone wanted one, I doubt there are any left in Kenya.

Nowadays, a mother carries a baby in her arms or, on long distances, ties the baby to her back with a piece of cloth.

But ngoi is alive and well elsewhere.

In California, United States, a person just needs to stroll around in pleasant weather, especially in summer, to see men and women carry their offspring in ngoi replicas, now with straps across the carrier's back or chest.

It is likely someone in the West has been credited with "inventing" ngoi centuries after the Gĩkũyũ mothers.

Chapter 14

Work Perks

Although I thought of little to tell my mother, I enjoyed accompanying her to her job and having her to myself, especially because Baby Morry slept most of the time and rarely cried. I also enjoyed listening to stories that women shared, sometimes shouted across several rows of coffee bushes.

Some women sang while others, mainly mothers with young children, concentrated on their work to make up for the feeding interruptions.

Women outnumbered men about three to one. Although men made occasional comments, I never heard them engage in long-winded conversations as women did. Sometimes, when women-talk or babies' cries became excessive, I heard comments like, "These women!"

Some mothers carried babies on their backs; others brought their budding coffee cherry-picker trainees, my age or older. These trainees carried little pails and picked from branches closer to the ground.

I never felt lonely, but sometimes I became weary of grownup talk and activity all day long. And surrounded by tall green bushes with little else to see dulled my mind. At such times, I longed to play with my sister, Tabitha. But I kept my thoughts to myself.

When we first arrived in the morning, we found Baba assigning rows of coffee bushes to pickers as they arrived. I heard him speak from time to time as he walked about.

At lunchtime, he came to Mother's row to get food that she carried for him in a small kîondo. She did this when they worked at the same plantation. But most days Baba carried his own lunch to wherever his work took him.

Late afternoon, Baba told the pickers to stop for the day. Some pickers trailed behind to grab one more fistful of coffee cherries. He then shooed and corralled them like he did goats at home.

"You got to go now!" he said as he walked along the rows of coffee bushes.

People referred to Baba as *nyapara*, overseer, a position he held during all my formative years.

At the coffee factory, people staked their spots on the grassy lot. Mother chose a prime spot close to the receptacle.

"Who wants to walk far carrying a tin full of coffee," she said.

The sprawl looked like an open-air market or a swap meet that Kenyans now call *Jua Kali (*hot sun), implying low-income workers who labor under the scorching sun.

People caused a lot of commotion before they settled down. Women called their stray children, babies cried, and the five-gallon tins clanked as each picker took one from near the receptacle.

When people settled in their spots, they spread sacks on the ground, poured pyramids of coffee cherries at one end, and sat at the other. They then picked out leaves or unripe ones before they put the cherries in tins, ready for inspection.

Pickers forfeited half a tin of ripe cherries or a full tin if the unripe ones were excessive. They paid no penalty if the unripe cherries were negligible, as most were. They put those in a sack placed near the receptacle platform.

When pickers became satisfied their coffee would pass the overseer's scrutiny, they filled their tins and carried them to the receptacle. Men held their loads high on their shoulders and women hugged theirs in front of their bodies. They passed by Baba, who stood by the platform.

The receptacle was a sloping concrete structure, about fifteen feet in diameter and four feet up from the ground. At the top, it rounded in front and tapered gradually toward the back, ending in a narrow opening at the lowest point.

This first inspection ensured the pickers had not tampered with tins. To stretch pickings, sometimes, a picker pressed in the four sides of a tin, or he or she skimped on the topping where cherries needed to pyramid.

(Years later, the farm owner ordered that cherries level at the rims for easier monitoring.)

If the overseer noticed the sides of a tin pressed inward or coffee not topped as required, he rejected the coffee. The picker then had to correct the infraction before his or her coffee passed inspection. When the overseer approved the cherries, the picker emptied the tin on the receptacle's surface.

But if the overseer caught a picker with unripe coffee cherries commingled with ripe ones inside the tin—invisible until poured—the penalty came fast. With his mere declaration, the picker forfeited the whole tin of coffee. People grumbled, but because no appeal existed, they did better the next round. Only gamblers took such chances, especially when it got too busy.

If the poured coffee cherries turned out okay, a picker progressed to the payment stage where Kamunge threw a shilling into the emptied tin.

Meanwhile, two barefoot men, trousers hitched up to their knees, stood on the receptacle's surface with huge brushes. They prodded laggard cherries to prevent them from backing up while they cascaded down to the bottom and disappeared into the bowels of the factory.

The reddish berries came out skinless, sticky, beige coffee beans on the other end. The beans next progressed to a station where the machine spun and washed them in plenty of water, and then spat them out, ready for people to dry them outside over flatbeds.

*

On our way home, the distance seemed longer than in the morning. Tired, I labored to walk behind my mother; she slowed her steps so I could keep up. But, no matter how slowly she walked, many times I could not catch up with her, especially when I frolicked if I got attracted by a plant or ran my hand through the tall wiregrass or walked zigzag. She had to wait for me from time to time.

"We would walk all night if you led and set the pace," she said.

That would scare me if it got dark because of my slowness, I thought.

"It's better if an adult leads," she said, "to clear the footpath."

I felt safer and taken care of when she said that.

*

Even after Morry's belly button healed, Mother still carried him at her front. On her back, she carried her coffee-picking paraphernalia or a kîondo with maize and vegetables she picked if we passed by our garden. By then, our maize was ready. She covered the kîondo with the now-empty coffee gunnysacks.

Through the savanna, we walked on a narrow footpath with wire grass and scrubs on both sides. With Mother ahead of me, she blocked my view ahead. But I did not realize the disadvantage, though, because my life revolved around her.

But I could see beyond her through one side where the footpath widened. It gave me a measure of freedom to flex my little body because I did not have to walk in a straight line.

One day, it started raining when we reached the middle of the savanna. Raindrops dripped down my face, and I could not wipe them fast enough. The wiregrass flattened and collapsed in parts of the footpath. Whenever I came by such a spot, my six-year-old feet could not sweep through the soaked, heavy grass. I raised my legs higher and stepped on top. I struggled and faltered with every step. Then a scatter of furious hailstones started to fall.

I had never seen hailstones rain before, or maybe I had and had forgotten.

Mother turned back and waited.

"This rain is too heavy for you," she said.

That seemed obvious to me.

When I reached her, she nuzzled me in front of her.

I started walking, surprised she wanted me to lead and then we might take all night to get home.

Now, hailstones bounced off my head and it hurt.

"Wait," she said, held my shoulder, and pulled me next to her.

I turned and looked up at my mother, unsure whether she wanted us to wait for the rain to ebb while she shielded me.

She hurriedly removed two empty gunnysacks from the top of the kîondo on her back.

"This rain is too heavy for you," she said.

She said that steps ago. What did she want me to do?

"I'll have to carry you."

Wow! What a treat!

I raised my arms, the one time I recall doing so. She always had too many hands raised toward her. Besides the baby, who else could she give such attention to? I had my chance and I grabbed it.

"You don't have to raise your arms," Mother said, then turned me around. From my back, she clasped her hands under my armpits and lifted me. She could not do it fast enough. By then, hailstones the size of marbles littered the footpath.

Mother deposited me on top of the kîondo and nudged me into position. My legs straddled her body around her ribcage, while my chin rested close to her collarbone. Satisfied, she covered me with the empty sacks.

The heavy rain and hailstones beat on my back and made rhythmic sounds that sounded like a lullaby. Soothed, I fell asleep within minutes. I woke up when she unloaded me at home. My dress crumpled, but my body all toasty.

I developed a lifelong happy memory of nurturing warmth and wellbeing. If I could choose one best childhood memory, I recall this incident with a special fondness for my mother.

FAMILY, MARRIAGES & ABUSE

Chapter 15

Polygamy

One legend is that the Gĩkũyũ nation started as a matriarchal system, a time women ruled over the land and fought wars like the Dahomey Amazon warriors. The community is even said to have practiced polyandry, meaning a woman could marry multiple husbands at the same time.

According to the legend, women rulers applied harsh, authoritarian rules that included capital punishment for philanderers.

Men persevered and remained in the good graces of their wives and community. But they reached a point where they could not bear the tyranny any longer. They planned a covert takeover.

One by one, they got their wives pregnant. While the women rulers wrestled with their hormones, morning sickness, and ballooning bodies, the men revolted. They overthrew the administration and replaced it with the patriarchal system the Gĩkũyũ practice today.

The legend does not explain how women lost their land ownership or inheritance rights, or whether the community expected them to shoulder the same family responsibilities as men assumed after the coup.

After the power grab, men restructured the system and outlawed polyandry. Instead, they introduced polygamy, which meant a man could marry multiple wives at the same time, provided he could afford to pay bride price.

Society also expected a man to provide land and a stable homestead for his wife or wives and children. If he slackened or failed to meet his obligations, his social status diminished. More than that, male members of his agemates ostracized him.

Agemates were young men and women who became of age and went through circumcision rites of passage at the same period.

Each *riika* (age group) had a formal name, the method Agĩkũyũ marked their ages and milestones in history.

Kĩhiũ Mwĩrĩ in 1913 was my father's age group, which he shared with Jomo Kenyatta, the first president of Kenya. (Men or women belonging to the same riika shared a lifelong bond similar to college fraternities or sororities. This means, if later in life Baba had met Mr. Kenyatta, and mentioned his riika, Mr. Kenyatta would have welcomed him and, at the very least, instructed his staff to treat Baba well.)

Unlike today, where some men misbehave and not feel beholden to their community, honor featured high in Gĩkũyũ tradition.

When a young man reached marriage age, he chose a young woman and then informed his father. The father, along with two friends, paid a visit and introduced the matter to the young woman's parents. Or, parents of the two young people arranged their marriage with their full knowledge. This joined and cemented the friendship between the two families.

If a man desired to marry an additional woman and had a prospect in mind, he consulted his first wife. He had no obligation to do so, but it nurtured harmony in their homestead.

If he had no particular woman in mind, his first wife helped scout for a suitable candidate. She approved additional marriages unless she had fallen out of favor with her husband, in which case he married whomever he chose.

In a polygamous home, in most cases, the senior wife commanded respect and ruled over the co-wife or co-wives.

Sometimes a polygamist wanted an additional wife and his wives objected. When that happened, the senior wife threw vocal tantrums about the peril of a new wife coming to disturb the serenity in their homestead. Except for tyrannical men, most husbands conceded and abandoned the idea.

Polygamy also came in handy if a husband fell out of love. He then married another woman and demoted his first wife to second-class status, or sexually ignored her. No wife had this option, even if she did not love her husband anymore. She stayed to raise her children.

When her son or sons matured and established their homesteads, behind their father's, one of them built a house for her.

*

There are varied reasons why Gĩkũyũ men practiced (and some still practice) polygamy: First, the more wives a man married, the more children he sired, the more work they performed, the more animals he owned, and the bigger the land he could own.

Polygamy was, therefore, a sign of wealth and prestige. Such men never did manual labor. They, instead, managed their animal herds and families. Display of wealth then, just like today, nourished and massaged men's egos and garnered a lot of power besides a possible esteemed seat in the governing council.

A man's standing and level of involvement in the community depended on whether he had a wife or wives and children. No Gĩkũyũ man could play a role in governance without a family.

And men dreaded to end up heirless. Polygamy removed this concern and ensured a man's lineage continued through his sons.

When daughters married, they joined their husbands' families, while sons became pillars of their families, clans, and community. If a man died without a son to take over as *mũramati na mũtungatĩri* (trustee and manager), his family line ended. To avoid this possibility, parents produced as many children as they could to ensure enough sons survived to continue the family bloodline.

Polygamy also came in handy in cases of infertility.

If a first wife did not become pregnant for an extended period, she anguished. Meanwhile, her in-laws complained their son married a *thata* (barren woman), while the community, especially the women, showered her with pity, implied or behind her back. Eventually, the husband married a second wife.

Most times, the infertile wife helped choose a young woman whom she believed would fit well in their prospective polygamous family.

When the co-wife bore children, both wives raised them together, and the children added an adjective after *maitũ* (mother) to differentiate between the two: *maitũ mũkũrũ* (senior mother) or a plain *maitũ* to refer to their birth mother. If their father married another wife, the children referred to her as *maitũ mũnyinyi* (junior mother).

Because there was no family without children, polygamy minimized or removed the stigma of infertility in cases of sterile women.

As regards male infertility, if a man married a second wife when his first wife failed to get pregnant, and the new wife failed to conceive for an extended period also, whispers about the man's fertility festered.

But wives with infertile husbands knew how to improvise and bring forth children through surrogacy. They, like other young men and women, learned about sexuality and infertility in their mid and late teens during rites of passage.

If a wife took too long to act, her mother-in-law nudged her.

"There is no difference between my son and his agemate," she said, implying it was about time the daughter-in-law chose a surrogate father among her husband's agemates.

The suitable man so chosen obliged and shut his mouth not to embarrass her husband.

Children so sired never learned the man who raised them was not their biological father. The adoptive father may have suspected, especially if the children resembled the surrogate. But such a father kept his suspicions to himself, happy he had a family and his infertility remained private.

Gĩkũyũ community never considered wives bearing children with their husbands' agemates as infidelity, shameful, or dishonorable. It fulfilled a need just like today's surrogacy or sperm donors.

Another reason for polygamy was the death of a spouse. Unlike today, Gĩkũyũ people did not practice single parenthood. A widower soon remarried and vice versa.

If a husband died, his wife married her brother-in-law. If her late husband had no brothers, she married a widower, and the two merged their families, or someone married her as his second wife.

Polygamy also curbed men's infidelity, especially when their first wives reached menopause. Men itched to marry second wives, while first wives longed to "retire." The wives had no illusions about their sexual prowess and happily helped court suitable wife candidates for their husbands to consider and marry.

Since men remained tight-lipped about the reasons for their plural marriages, I never heard a single man discuss his pure selfish motive.

It was an open secret that, despite the high-value men placed on children, they found them bothersome before those children grew old enough to run errands, herd animals, or work the land. Sometimes a man married a second wife to get away from his first wife's hectic child-rearing.

When the second wife bore children, and the first wife's children were still dependent, the man might marry a third wife. By the time that wife got her own brood, the first wife's children would be grown. The man then weaseled back to his first wife and nurtured a closer liaison.

If a man could not afford bride price for multiple wives, he confined himself to *thingira*, the man cave sanctuary, which I suppose came about for that purpose.

*

Agĩkũyũ started phasing out polygamy after Britain invaded and occupied Kenya, which resulted in smaller lands and taxation. The government levied the so-called *Hut Tax* based on the number of houses in a man's homestead.

The more wives a man married, the more houses, and the more taxes he paid.

To raise the needed money, men left their families behind and trekked long distances away from their communities in search of work. They found jobs on European farms and in towns, which made mobility and unstable living conditions another polygamy deterrent.

Today, although polygamous Gĩkũyũ families are uncommon, one can still spot an occasional husband with two wives. And although women are against polygamy, a minority still supports it.

Some people claim these women are mistresses who want the law to help them emerge from the shadows.

It's hard to understand these women's concerns because, as of this writing, Muslim and Customary (tribal) Marriages are polygamous under Kenyan law. A man can marry multiple wives as long as he follows the set procedures and no person objects when he applies for registration.

*

My father wrestled with polygamy for about fifteen years, but failed to thrive in it. Otherwise, on both sides of my family, from my great grandparents to this day, no one else has indulged in polygamous unions.

Chapter 16

Kaguyu

Baba and his first wife, Kaguyu, married about a year before World War I ended. They lived on the plot at Kahiga-inî in Nyeri that Baba, as a teenager, carved out and cleared from the community's lands, before the British took them over.

Similar to other young men in the community, he planned to establish a home and raise a family.

But to his and Kaguyu's anguish, several years passed without her getting pregnant.

Meanwhile, they learned of a famine in Meru, where they could get a female child for a sack of maize—boy children were not for sale. When they made up their minds to buy a child, Baba consulted travelers who told him of an old woman (who I'll call Kendi) who accommodated lodgers. He sent word that he and his wife would arrive at her home within the month.

After two weeks. Baba and his bride in the company of other travelers trekked to Meru, about 50 miles away. He carried the sack of maize while Kaguyu carried the supplies they needed during their safari.

They plodded along a well-traveled footpath through a wilderness of trees and thick underbrush inhabited by elephants, leopards, buffaloes, wild hogs, and other animals.

They rested at dusk and slept in turns next to bonfires they built from dead tree branches, not only to keep warm but also to ward off animals they heard growl and grunt at night.

With heavy loads, it took them a week to arrive at Kendi's house.

The following day, they accompanied someone to an intermediary's homestead. After they exchanged pleasantries in the man's thingira, another man helped Baba carry the sack of maize from where he left it in the courtyard. He scooped the amount of maize required, using the two-mug *mūraũri* (goblet with white interior and blue exterior) that Baba had carried for that purpose.

The intermediary then sent for the biological parents to bring their young daughter so Baba and Kaguyu could see her.

The girl looked about four years old, which the prospective parents liked. They had already agreed to get the youngest child available, who they planned to pamper until she forgot her parents and her previous life.

The girl's biological father told Baba and Kaguyu to fetch their new daughter the following morning.

When they returned, they found the so-called biological father and another man waiting in the intermediary's thingira. Baba joined the men while Kaguyu waited, seated on the granary's jutting boards. "The girl is in nyŭmba," the intermediary said.

Since Baba had settled the matter with the men the previous day, he wanted to collect his new daughter and leave.

The biological father called out to his wife to bring the girl. When the woman entered, a much older girl followed behind, biting on her fingers, head bent sideways.

"This is not the same child!" Baba said.

"What's the difference?" the intermediary asked. "A child is a child."

"What happened to the one you brought us yesterday?"

"She's not available anymore."

"My wife and I came all this way to deal with lying grown men?"

"Return the child to nyŭmba," the man told the woman. "We'll call when we need you."

Baba finished his complaints by calling the men sneaky and dishonorable.

The men did not protest or explain their behavior.

"I have to discuss this with my wife," Baba said.

Outside, he and Kaguyu talked at the side of thingira.

"We want a young child," Baba said when he rejoined the group. "But I didn't bring my wife all this way to return empty-handed. We'll take the girl."

"Things are not good," the intermediary said. "The mother changed her mind and left with the girl."

Baba and the child-sellers exchanged heated words that, under a different setting, would have resulted in a fistfight.

Crushed, he and Kaguyu left in disgust.

*

On their second trip, Baba and Kaguyu got swindled again.

After the transaction, whoever they sent to bring the girl claimed a relative took her away.

When they returned to Nyeri, Baba and Kaguyu shared their ordeal with their neighbors. They said they could not understand why the children's parents changed their minds or became sneaky and hostile.

Because they spoke only little *Kimeru*, they figured they could have misunderstood the amount of maize required.

On their third and last trip, the couple carried a bigger sack of maize in case that was the problem.

Just like before, Kaguyu's load became lighter as they depleted their supplies. She was not too tired when they arrived at Kendi's house. But when Baba dropped his heavy sack, he felt so drained and fatigued he could not sit upright. Kendi showed him a plank bed to stretch and rest. He slept for two days and awoke on the afternoon of the third day.

"When I awoke," he said, decades later, "it was as if I came out from a coma."

After Baba ate and rested for another day, he and Kaguyu went to see the girl at her parents' homestead. When Baba said they brought a sack of maize, the father balked. For his daughter, the man said, he wanted the sack to contain equal amounts of maize and *njahî* (white-eyed peas).

Baba became so stupefied he could not verbalize his discontent. Defeated, he shook his head, turned, and walked away. Kaguyu clicked her tongue and followed her husband.

Back at Kendi's house, Baba sat and hung his head.

When Kendi learned the reason Baba looked so distraught, she showered him with blessings.

"Don't worry, Warama," she said. "Children will fill your home to the brim like this," she clapped her hands to seal her prediction.

To Baba, Kendi's words sounded such nonsense. He took her for a senile old crone and waved his hand toward her dismissively.

Kendi repeated her prediction.

"Come on," Baba said to Kaguyu. "Get ready. We'll leave early morning."

After supper that evening, Kaguyu talked sense into her husband. They rested for another two days before they joined another group of travelers headed back to Nyeri.

On the way, Baba and Kaguyu lamented their fruitless endeavor. He said they would never try to buy a child again. As they wrangled with the idea of how they would lead a childless life, Baba said, to ease their burden, they would become "*athomi*" (readers), like some of their neighbors.

Nothing seemed to face athomi people. To them, everything was the will of God.

During that period, European missionaries campaigned with fervor to convert Gĩkũyũ people to Christianity.

They referred to those who practiced Gĩkũyũ religion as *plain* Agĩkũyũ and those who converted to Christianity as

Athomi. This meant "the people who read the bible," and, of course, attended church.

When Baba and Kaguyu returned home, Baba declared the goblet he used to scoop maize a family heirloom, and stored it in his trunk.

Kaguyu started attending church sporadically. But Baba took time to come around. But he stopped his frowns or any mean comment about the foreign religion.

By the year's end, as if infertility was not enough burden, Kaguyu suffered from stomach problems. Sometimes she became so sick she stayed home. Her stomach bloated all the time.

Helpless, Baba kept mum about the misfortune that weighed on him. No baby and now a sick wife? It could be a woman's issue, he consoled himself, caused by too many thoughts about a baby.

When Kaguyu kept up her complaints, Baba blamed it on food. But after she avoided the foods she suspected and even drank herbal soups to cleanse her stomach, the sickness persisted.

Finally, Kaguyu consulted the wise women of the village before she paid a visit to a medicine man.

While the women tossed their ideas around, one woman suggested she give Kaguyu a massage.

In a minute, the masseuse burst out laughing.

"Don't tell me you didn't suspect," the woman said after her laughter played out.

"Suspect what?"

"You are suffering from pregnancy."

"Are you sure?" Kaguyu whispered.

"Of course, I'm sure," the woman replied. "You know how many children I have brought forth?"

Kaguyu could not return home fast enough to tell her husband.

Lo-and-behold, in four months, the couple welcomed their first baby girl, Wanjirū-big, named after Baba's mother. They trailed off from their *Athomi* path before Baba got around to attending church.

In another two years, the happy couple welcomed a boy (Njerū-big) named after Baba's father and then another, Waigwa, named after Kaguyu's father. They became overjoyed with their good fortune.

*

Over the years, Baba reminisced about their quest and marveled at Kendi's prediction. But he never said how long he and Kaguyu tried to buy a child. The period spanned between four and seven years, depending on who told the story.

But when I interviewed my mother for a college paper, she told me they stayed childless for six years.

Kaguyu had become so used to her childless state that she once forgot her infant daughter in the garden and realized it only after she arrived home.

My half-sister, Gathoni, told me in June 2016 that besides going to Meru, Baba and Kaguyu (her mother) had gone to solicit for a child near Lake Baringo, an area populated by Kalenjin people.

But I never heard that story before my parents died and I could not get another relative—all younger than Gathoni—to confirm it.

Chapter 17

Bonus Son

While infertility and family distracted Warama and Kaguyu, the social upheaval in the country ranged on.

As the colonized, they, like their community, still had to obey the new laws and adapt to the colonial culture.

When the British turned Kenya into a protectorate in 1895, they introduced a cash economy—a replica of the English system— to replace the previous currency and barter system that the natives used.

The colonial government now required each man to pay taxes in British shillings and pounds, termed "hut tax," a tax based on the number of houses he had in his homestead.

Before then, men worked on their land, took care of their families, livestock, and community, and traded with neighboring micro-nations.

The monumental change weighed heavily on heads of households. They had no choice but to change their lifestyles and work for their colonizers in order to take part in the new economy and afford to pay taxes.

Tax collectors' jobs became harder and harder when they visited the community to collect taxes or apprehend those who could not pay. Sometimes the government confiscated livestock in place of money. When men resisted, the taxman and his assistants turned to threats or physical violence.

The new cash economy and taxation caused many men to abandon their families and flee in search of work in towns or on British-owned farms.

They returned home every few months, or once every year, to visit and take money home to their families.

The practice of fathers living away from their families persisted up to the 1970s when men returned home at the end of each month after payday.

Separation of husbands from their wives and children—alien to Gĩkũyũ community—created absentee fathers. Men became alienated from family relationships and their communities, which led many of them, especially in towns, to undesirable activities that resulted in transmitted diseases. It also turned many wives into heads of households.

Baba got caught up in that migrants' wave when he failed to convince the tax collector that he had no money to pay. Orphaned as a teenager, the oldest of four children, he and his family owned little that the tax collector could seize for payment of taxes. In the ensuing argument, one assistant hit Baba with a baton on his hip.

The altercation became Baba's breaking point.

In the mid-1920s, he could not stand living in Nyeri, his homeland. He left his wife, Kaguyu, and three young children—a girl and two boys—and joined a migrant workers' caravan headed west toward the Great Rift Valley.

The men trudged on footpaths through virgin land, going from farm to farm in search of work.

Baba found a job at Kamunge's farm in Solai, Nakuru County.

Kamunge was a nickname given to the British farm manager by his workers because they did not know his name or could not pronounce it.

After Baba proved his worth, he asked Kamunge for a plot to build a homestead. With the help of fellow laborers, he built his thingira at Kĩrĩma-inĩ. After he moved from the migrant workers' camp he shared with his workmates, he built a similar but larger house for his wife, Kaguyu.

I have no information about how long it took Baba to stabilize and return to Nyeri to fetch his family. But when he returned, he found four children instead of the three he left. How he reacted remains buried with the departed. But he and his wife settled the matter. He accepted the boy—a bonus son who Kaguyu had named after her brother, Werũ.

Meanwhile, Baba stayed, winding down his affairs in Nyeri, long enough to stray. He would learn later the woman he partnered with in Ragati Location brought forth a baby boy she named Mwangi (after Baba).

Decades later, my brother Simon met the half-brother—a middle-aged man. According to Simon, the man resembled Baba. He, Simon, also said he heard rumors that my father would have married the mother as a second wife, but she did not seem a good wife candidate.

Given Baba's situation then, I doubt he could have afforded to marry her.

Instead, he bundled his family and turned his back on Gĩkũyũland.

His infidelity and the son who resulted from it remained a blip, nothing worthy of mention in the family. I learned of the incident in my middle-age years.

Baba's long absence, however, and both of their infidelities started the quakes between him and his wife, which clouded their marriage for the rest of its duration.

*

At Kamunge's farm, Kaguyu could not settle down. To unsettle her even more, she gave birth to a baby boy—Mwai—who died in infancy.

In time, though, the two ended up with five sons—Njerũ, Waigwa, Werũ, Mwai, and Gĩthũi; and three girls—Wanjirũ, Gathoni, and Wairimũ. (Except for Mwai, the others lived well into their 80s and the remaining three have reached the 90s mark.)

But, despite producing more children than they ever expected, and which confirmed Kendi's prediction, the couple's marriage never thrived again.

Over the years, the husband and wife became opposites. They disagreed on almost everything. For example: If Kaguyu said she would wait to tend to her crops after the rain stopped, Baba would claim those were only droplets, an excuse for sloths to avoid work and stay home.

Tired of their wobbly marriage, in 1936, Baba escaped to the arms of another woman.

Chapter 18

Nyacuru

Before colonization fragmented the Gĩkũyũ nation, every year young men and women went through rites of passage known as *riika*, age group. They engaged in songs, dances, and socialized with each other. Willing partners practiced safe sex known as *ngwĩko*, a type of masturbation.

A man gyrated his hips and rubbed his member on his partner's oiled thighs until he ejaculated. Tradition forbade the *lucky* men from tampering with the chastity belts young women wore. But sometimes a young man lost control and forced his way in.

Or a young woman got carried away and joined in her mate's enthusiasm. But the blame fell on the man because society believed women were feeble-minded.

If the woman accused her partner of crossing the line of decency, the young man suffered the consequences when his agemates and community ostracized him.

If the young woman became pregnant, the partners married. But sometimes the man denied responsibility and refused to marry her, and instead forced her into a trial. But no woman became pregnant and refused to marry the responsible party. Otherwise, her father married her off as a second wife. Unlike today, society did not tolerate single motherhood.

In the early twentieth century, *ngwîko* practice died off because of migration to farms or towns or to war where people lived among communities of different cultures.

Even in homogenous communities like Nyeri, customs and traditional safeguards lost their potency, replaced by the new colonial laws which did not apply to natives' basic concerns. Instead, wrongdoers did not have to remain beholden to their communities. They left and got work elsewhere among unknown, diverse people.

Those were the main circumstances in *Tŭmŭtŭmŭ*, Nyeri County, under which Nyandia, the woman who would later become my maternal grandmother, brought forth her Oops child in or about 1910.

Most likely, a young man forced himself onto Nyandia and disappeared when he learned of the outcome. Except for the child, the incident remained a family secret. The few members of Nyandia's family who knew what happened are long dead.

Back then, bearing a child out of wedlock resulted in enormous embarrassment for Nyandia and her family. They sealed their lips and pretended nothing out of the ordinary happened. Nyandia gave birth and named her little Oops Nyokabi after her mother.

*

"Nyokabi" means from *ũkabi* or Maasai. The adoptive family gave the name to my great-great-grandmother when warriors captured her from the Maasai nation as war booty, after Gĩkũyũ and Maasai's livestock raid. (Gĩkũyũ Nation never harmed females when they went to war with their neighbors. The worst they did was capture young girls and absorb them into the tribe.)

The Maasai may have practiced the same. My brother Simon told me of an ancient Maasai woman he met when he worked in Narok in the 1970s. When his workmate took him to visit their Maasai *boma* (homestead), Simon met the old woman basking in the sun, seated next to a wall. Besides nodding when his colleague introduced his grandmother, Simon could not talk to her because she spoke no Kiswahili.

Halfway through his visit, Simon loafed around the yard because it was his first time to visit a boma. The woman beckoned him.

"Umîte mwena *ũrîkũ* wa Gĩkũyũ?" (Which area of Gĩkũyũland are you from?) the woman asked.

Surprised, Simon hesitated.

"I'm from Nakuru," he said. How did you learn to speak Gĩkũyũ?

The old woman chuckled. "I became a Maasai as a young girl," she said.

*

Baby Nyokabi grew up to a healthy toddler and became a handful. Her grandmother and other women claimed the little girl rushed *curu, curu, curu, curu* (here, there, here, there). In time, the women concocted the name *Nyacuru*, a busybody who does the *curu*.

*

As it occasionally happened in that era, if a young woman became pregnant out of wedlock and did not marry the responsible party (who may have paid a fine or taken off), she married an older married man or a widower.

Nyandia beat the odds when she married a single man by the name of Ndurumo, son of Kĩbacwa and Kagendo. When her daughter, Nyokabi, aka Nyacuru, reached an age to know who-was-who around her household, Ndurumo was the father she found.

After Nyandia married Ndurumo, she suffered several miscarriages. But in 1923, she bore Nyacuru a brother, my uncle, Eliud "Njoroge" Machira Ndurumo.

When Machira reached three or four years old, his family left Nyeri for a better life in the Rift Valley. On their way, the parents left him and his sister at their maternal uncle's home at a colonial farm in Nanyuki. They planned to fetch the children after they got work and stabilized.

Ndurumo and Nyandia found work at Major Holman's (Horoma's) farm, east of *Kamunge*'s farm. *They* returned to Nanyuki and picked up little Machira, but left Nyacuru. She may not have known why her parents left her behind because she never mentioned it.

Later in her teens, Nyacuru left her uncle's and joined her family at Horoma's. My uncle was too young to know who decided his sister should rejoin the family. Although based on Ndurumo's later behavior, he may have decided.

If he left Nyacuru to become of age at her uncle's, it was likely the uncle would receive the bride price when she married. I doubt Ndurumo wanted to take that chance. Except for his one young son who would expect help with bride price when his time came to marry, Ndurumo had no other daughters. He, therefore, needed to have Nyacuru under his own roof.

As Nyacuru matured, she fetched water, cut and hauled firewood on her back, gardened, and helped in other household chores. She also picked pyrethrum at Horoma's and coffee cherries at the neighboring farms to the west. It so happened that one farm where she picked coffee cherries was Kamunge's, where Baba worked as an overseer.

Baba noticed and admired Nyacuru's work ethic from afar. This coincided with his search for a good wife candidate to insulate himself from his turbulent first marriage. After he observed Nyacuru for a while, learned of her identity, and checked on her character, the chase was on.

Nyacuru could not stand Baba's advances, not only because he looked much older than she but also because she learned he had a wife.

From a young age, Nyacuru had observed a polygamous family next door where the senior wife ruled over her much younger junior co-wife as if the senior wife were the mother or the husband. She also heard women talk about authoritarian senior co-wives. When she became of age, she promised herself she would never become a co-wife.

But Baba refused to quit. Whenever he tried to talk to her, however, Nyacuru groaned or ignored him altogether.

One time she walked through the grassland when she saw a man at a distance. When he reached about fifty feet from her and she recognized Baba, she rushed several yards inland to avoid walking near him.

When he reached parallel to where she stood, he wiggled his index finger at her and said, "Ndurumo's daughter, one day you'll become my wife."

She muffled a laugh.

"You'll see."

She returned to the footpath after he walked a distance away.

*

Baba was no catch. He was about twenty years older than Nyacuru—an older, married man, the exact type of man Nyacuru had sworn not to marry. No man in her family had married more than one wife.

But Baba kept at it, waiting for Nyacuru to come around. If she remained stubborn, he, Warama son of Njerũ, would find a way to marry her.

She remained stubborn. With no other option, Baba bypassed Nyacuru and sent a message to Ndurumo that he, Warama, wanted to "visit" the family, a code meaning he wanted to ask for Nyacuru's hand in marriage.

On the agreed date, Baba and his entourage of three men traveled to Ndurumo's homestead. Warama's hopes rose when they arrived. Ndurumo owned a small homestead, which contained three houses—thingira, nyũmba, a granary, and a small goats' cottage—a sign of a man who could give in to persuasion to increase his herd.

After Ndurumo and two of his friends welcomed the visitors, the group sat in his thingira where women who helped Mrs. Ndurumo cook served them. When the men finished eating and the women cleared the dishes, Warama's representative opened the formal proceedings.

"My colleagues and I came to introduce ourselves," the man said, "and to ask you to allow the daughter of this homestead to join Warama's homestead."

"We welcome you to this homestead," Ndurumo said.

After about a minute of such exchanges, as it's customary, Ndurumo needed to consult his daughter before he started the actual proceedings.

"Machira," he called out to his young son. "Go tell your sister to come."

Nyacuru entered and stood by the side of the doorway.

Ndurumo pointed, "This man's name is Warama," he said. "Do you know him?"

"Yes," Nyacuru said.

"He came to this homestead because of you," Ndurumo said. "Before I discuss anything with him, I want to confirm. Do you agree to marry him?"

"No," she said. "He has another wife."

Ndurumo squinted at Nyacuru, paused for seconds that made it clear to all present that was not the answer he expected. Then he said, "You can go now."

That'll show him—coming here while he knows I don't want him, Nyacuru told herself on her way out.

She could not wait to tell her mother how she embarrassed Warama in front of the men. She had become appalled by his audacity when he sent a message that he intended to visit, but more so when he and his group entered the courtyard.

"That man has no shame," Nyacuru said to her mother. "I've told him over and over I don't want to marry him. What did he expect?"

"What did your father say?"

"Nothing."

"Nothing at all?"

"What could he say? I don't want to marry a married man."

*

Nyacuru's sunny and industrious disposition worked against her. The old and the young admired her. Men preferred her type—fertile, out-going women who did not flinch at hard work.

But the young admirers she hoped to marry did not own goats or money. Without well-to-do fathers to help them with bride price, they promised to pay in installments.

But Warama son of Njerũ was ready and eager to shell out the total bride price.

It depressed Ndurumo to think he could pass such an opportunity.

About three years prior, he had listened to one of those bride-price-installment young men. Things did not end up well.

Why would he miss a chance to boost his meager herd? He would also get a lump sum of shillings, an amount he had never managed to save.

Ndurumo was no workaholic. He watched over people who picked pyrethrum or did other errands on the farm. The man shunned manual labor as if it were an infectious disease. He never even helped his wife to cultivate the piece of land where his family grew food.

As the first son of Kĩbachwa, and the looker in the family, Ndurumo towered over his brothers—who were at least 5 feet 10 inches themselves. He displayed symmetrical features and soft hands with long manicured nails, a relic of a Gĩkũyũ elder.

Similar to many men of that era, he controlled his homestead with a firm hand.

So Nyacuru's rejection of Warama did not slow Ndurumo. He entertained his future son-in-law and his friends as if Nyacuru said "yes" to the marriage.

After the men left, Ndurumo talked to his wife.

"You better talk to your daughter," he told her. "Those men didn't visit this homestead to waste their time."

"What did she say?" Nyandia asked.

"I said to talk to her."

Nyandia got caught up between her husband and her daughter. Like many wives in those days, she knew her husband's word was final. She did not, therefore, dare attempt to change his mind.

Her out-of-wedlock pregnancy, miscarriages, and deaths of multiple children, besides her husband's narcissism, weakened her position in the marriage. Sometimes, Ndurumo implied she was lucky he married her.

But despite Ndurumo's heavy-handedness, Nyacuru remained steadfast.

Chapter 19
It is a Man's World

As a young woman, Nyacuru vowed never to become a junior wife, let alone marry an older man. With her outgoing disposition, she believed only a lesser woman agreed to become a co-wife and live under the shadow of the senior wife.

She planned to love and marry a man in her age group, a man who cherished monogamy. But if her husband later married a second wife, she figured, at least she would occupy the respected first wife's slot.

Nyacuru was ahead of her time in thinking her tantrums or marriage ideals mattered to Ndurumo.

Ndurumo, son of Kîbachwa, scoffed at what he called *wendo* foolishness. To him, love would develop after marriage. If it did not, oh well, Nyacuru would still have an established husband to provide for her and her future children. And he, Ndurumo, would have the bride price—goats and a wad of shillings—to show for it.

But Nyacuru overlooked those benefits and remained adamant in her resolve.

Meanwhile, whenever Warama and his entourage sent a message requesting a second visit, Ndurumo claimed he was not ready to receive them. The excuses implied a man who lacked control over his own homestead.

Embarrassed and troubled by how he seemed to his potential son-in-law, Ndurumo vowed to nudge his daughter to change her mind.

But how would he do that short of beating her?

In Gĩkũyũ tradition, however, the discipline of a daughter fell on the mother. Therefore, Ndurumo could do nothing except either give up or turn on his wife.

"Did you talk to your daughter?" he started, followed by verbal abuse accusing his wife of failing in her duties.

When that failed, Ndurumo turned to physical violence. Not a week passed without verbal or physical violence toward his wife.

The violence in her home tortured Nyacuru. She felt cornered and cried for her mother. Yet, her mother endured the beatings and never once pressured her daughter to change her mind. The guilt agonized Nyacuru even more.

"I felt as much pain as if he were beating me," she later said.

In time, Nyacuru felt responsible for her mother's suffering. No one else could stop it but her.

Her resolve shook, and she agreed to the marriage proposal.

She and Baba married in late 1936.

*

The following year, Baba took Nyacuru to meet his sister Julia, who then worked as a nurse in Nairobi. He invited his oldest daughter—Wanjirũ-big—so she could keep Nyacuru company when his sister took him to visit her job or any places they could not go all together.

Baba likely intended to console his new bride and to prove he was a better provider than any of those poor, snotty young men she wanted to marry.

For their first major outing, Aunt Julia arranged with a doctor she worked for to get them tickets to the Nairobi Ngong Racecourse, about three miles from the town center. Although Aunt Julia had told them how special those tickets were and what to expect, they did not understand it until they arrived.

Despite having *special* tickets, the gatekeepers told them to wait by the gate. Attendees gawked and frowned as they passed by the African guests. But a handful of them needed a more potent act than frowns. They zigzagged off the walkway to where the guests stood.

"Get out of the way," they said.

Aunt Julia and her guests waited until all the privileged entered.

Then they approached the gate where two men had just finished taking tickets.

"You can't come here," one man said.

But the good doctor already understood how low his tribe could stoop about sharing anything that would benefit the natives. He had gone before the official opening, talked to one gatekeeper, and signed his guests in.

During the back-and-forth exchange, one gatekeeper remembered about the sign-in and allowed Aunt Julia and company to enter.

As they entered, Baba in sandals, knee-high shorts, a shirt, a coat, and a hat, and Aunt Julia in a dress and shoes, and both used to dealing with white men, held their own. But Nyacuru and Wanjirũ-big in traditional clothes and shoeless, and having never seen more than two white people in one place, let alone a whole racecourse, behaved like timid little rural children. They looked around, frazzled and conspicuous in an all whites-only domain. Africans went there only to serve, clean the stables, and tend to the horses.

Meanwhile, the privileged stared, some turned from side-to-side alarmed as if a lion appeared in their midst and expecting someone to save them from an imminent attack.

The need to segregate the racecourse stands had never arisen, but each person present knew the colonial culture. So, neither the colonized nor the colonizers expected the three women and one man to proceed to the stands' empty seats.

After Aunt Julia's party endured the stares long enough, they realized they needed to figure it out for themselves. They picked a spot between stands and watched the races, standing or sitting on the grass.

After the racecourse visit, my parents' only satisfaction was that they trod where others could not dare and watched white people, all stiff with white or khaki clothes and hats, involved in a mundane activity. Otherwise, watching horses gallop or trot was a waste of their time, Mother said the one time I heard her mention the horses.

But they enjoyed one place—at least my mother did—when Aunt Julia took them to watch a dance at Kaloleni Hall east of the town center.

Years later, Mother said she had never seen such an impressive place. Music flowed from an accordion and *karing'aring'a,* a metal ring, while well-dressed people with polished black shoes slid around on the floor.

Hands in a prayer stance, she slid her palms, up-and-down, up-and-down, while she mouthed shhh—shhh—shhh smooth gliding sound the dancers' shoes made. At such a climax, Mother said, she never heard a single peep—only music and shoes massaging the cement floor.

She enjoyed *mwomboko* dance the most.

To dance mwomboko, dancers take long steps similar to a tango. At intervals, the men gyrate their partners' waists and lift them straight up, inches off the ground as if they were weightless, sometimes as high as a foot or two. (Men don't raise their partners while they dance on concrete—perhaps a couple of inches or so).

The Nairobi visit never lost its charm right up to Mother's waning years.

*

Despite her initial warm welcome to Warama's homestead, however, what Mother feared about a married man came true in her first year of marriage.

Within a short period, she realized Kaguyu and Baba led a combative life, and Kaguyu took off whenever the two fought. Mother had to step in to take care of her young step-children.

And she never changed her negative attitude about polygamy. When I became a young woman, she warned me against men with prior families.

Chapter 20

Wife Runaways

Traditionally, a wife ran to her parents when she became dissatisfied with her husband's conduct or tyrannical behavior, hoping he would change his ways.

When she arrived at her parents' homestead, however, the first thing her father asked her was: "Does your husband provide well for you and your children?"

The answer was usually "Yes," which meant she received little sympathy, especially from her father who, most likely indulged in the same behavior his daughter complained about.

Mother, thinking her case different, expected to garner sympathy when she took off after six years of marriage and already with two sons, David and Simon. She fumed, slung the almost three-year-old Simon on her back, secured him with a *ngoi* and a sheet, and ran to her parents at Horoma's, two farms away. She left her five-year-old David at the mercy of Baba and his first family.

Little Simon, aka Ndurumo—named after his grandfather—soon let his grandparents know he belonged to a different homestead. From the first day, he rushed close to the entrance when his grandfather's now bigger herd piled in from the day's grazing.

"Baba's goats!" he said, running to the courtyard. "Goats have come. Baba's goats come home."

To him, every goat belonged to his father.

By the third day, the elder Ndurumo had enough of the boy's utterances.

"Return this boy home to his father," Ndurumo said.

Mother never ran away again.

In telling us the story, she omitted the reason she abandoned her marriage. We never asked her either. My parents rarely told us their personal stories at length. When they did, we enjoyed the telling so much we never thought of asking questions.

Whatever the case, most wife-run-aways were mere protests, meant to punish husbands by showing them the home could not run as well or would collapse without their wives.

More times than not, a husband suppressed his pride and went to fetch his wife when managing a household bogged him down, and he could not bear the burden of an extra day without her.

But with a stubborn husband, too proud to concede, a wife got tired of waiting, swallowed her pride, and returned.

On arrival, she skulked in case the husband was home. She then eased into her house and started her usual chores. If the husband were home or when he returned, he pretended he never noticed her absence, and life went on.

*

Even in those days, my parents' marriage fell outside the norm. Fathers did not force their daughters into marriages. The only times they pressured daughters or sons to marry were in cases of out-of-wedlock pregnancies.

Otherwise, young men and women chose their mates or their parents arranged the marriages with full knowledge and agreement of the couples. Even in arranged marriages, the couple could opt-out.

*

When my siblings and I were little, on a rare occasion, to our utter pleasure, Baba came home drunk and, if Mother did or said something complimentary to him, he quipped, "I know I married a good woman." And then dived into one of the incidents of their so-called courtship.

If Mother commented with a different version, Baba threw back his own, and the two challenged each other in jest.

"All I'm trying to say is that I got myself a good wife," Baba would finally say.

"Me?" Mother would ask. "You have my father to thank."

"I said you'd be my wife, didn't I?" Baba would say, and throw her a sly look and a handful of knowing nods.

"Only because you colluded with my father."

"Tell me who got it right, eh?"

Mother would then snort and throw him an amused side-glance.

*

My mother thought highly of herself and kept her mouth zipped about issues that put her in bad light. I doubt she knew someone had entrusted me with a *just-between*-us whisper about her.

The tidbit hardly came up. But when it did, on very rare occasions, it was almost incidental between select family members only. I doubt most of my siblings learned of the whisper.

Before Baba, Mother had married Baiya, a bride price in-installment young man. Ndurumo had cursed his bad luck that he might join his ancestors before he received half of his bride price.

The young couple bore a son, who they named Gîthînji, after Baiya's father. For reasons that remain unknown, when Gîthînji turned a year old, Mother gathered him up and returned to her parents' home. Gîthînji died of high fever just months after Baba and Mother married. He was about two-and-a-half-years old.

Mother never breathed a word of her Oops birth or her short first marriage before she died.

When writing this book, her brother Machira, who was a young boy then and now in his late nineties, confirmed the story and gave me the names.

As for Kaguyu, even with a co-wife as a buffer, she and Baba failed to revive their withered union. After Mother and Baba married, Kaguyu took off several times and left her young children in the care of Nyacuru.

For the sake of the children, Kaguyu and Baba continued their Yo-Yo marriage for another ten years before it collapsed.

By then, two of their sons and one daughter had married and started their own families, the bonus son was in his twenties, the youngest son, Gîthũi-big, had gone with Aunt Julia, and the two youngest daughters were already teenagers.

Kaguyu and Baba separated in 1947.

Chapter 21

Nyambura

If the end of his first marriage brought Baba relief, it turned out short-lived. My mother's crowded household brought him another kind of stress. She had five children who all competed with him for her attention.

We, the brood, warmed ourselves by a campsite sort of fireplace, close to the center pillar in Nyũmba, where Mother cooked our food. Three sturdy masonry stone blocks supported a sizable pot. But the wear and tear from the fire left the blocks smaller and misshapen. A stone could tip over if someone stepped on it.

Once in a long while, Mother got a replacement or two at the farm's quarry where two stonecutters chiseled well-shaped building stone blocks. If cutters made mistakes, they liked it when the women scavenged for the stones so the boss would not see them if he stopped by.

Above the fireplace, *itara* (a raised wood platform) rested on four posts about seven feet high. Mother stored firewood there for when it became hard to keep wood dry during the rainy season. Otherwise, she kept piles next to her house or under the eaves.

With Mother's unending chores, she hurried to cook our evening meals. On the days she cooked red beans, which gave Baba indigestion, or if she thought Baba would frown on what she cooked for the day, she cooked a separate dish for him.

But between her job, gardening, and raising five children, she lacked the time to prepare palatable dishes for Baba, let alone the time to serve him.

After she ladled the food, one of my brothers took Baba his share. (Mother didn't take food to thingira anymore.) Joseph always rushed to volunteer. Before Mother knew better, she let him. In his hurry, he spilled or dropped Baba's food on two occasions. He still took it to him, with only half remaining on the plate.

"Return it to your mother," Baba would say.

That meant a double-duty for Mother as she hustled for another plate.

When she finished cooking the main meal, because of how anxious we waited for it, she did not wait for it to cool before she dished it out. She served us children on white enamel plates or bowls, starting with the youngest.

We placed our steaming servings on the floor beside us (or later in our laps) while we sat on the floor or on low stools. I ate from a little bowl or soup-type plate before my sister Tabitha grew old enough to share a plate with me.

My brothers—David, Simon, and Joseph (then known as Njerũ, Ndurumo, and Machira before they added the western names when we moved to the village) all ate from one plate. They gobbled their food as if in a competition.

They swished it in their mouths to cool it by taking air in between their teeth with a hiss. Joseph complained he could not keep up and urged his brothers to slow down. But they ignored his pleas.

The only time I saw him not complain about food was when Mother cooked *mataha* or *mũkimo* that lasted us for two to three days.

For my sister Tabitha or any other small child, Mother stirred food in a bowl and blew on every scoop before she fed it to her.

Baba could hear our chatter and commotion.

His thingira, at about 600 square feet, was smaller than Nyũmba. A wall across its center divided it into a sitting area and a bedroom, with the entrance at the center. Baba warmed himself by a fire similar to ours, which Mother kindled in the mornings and my brothers in the evenings.

When we all settled to eat, my brothers finished their food first, and then Joseph rushed to Baba's thingira to keep him company. Baba pretended he had eaten enough and gave Joseph leftovers.

"If Joseph weren't your son," Baba said to Mother once, "I would think you starve the boy."

Perhaps it never occurred to her to serve Joseph on a separate plate or that she cooked less than her family needed.

Baba must have reached a tipping point where he became tired of the noise and hungry mouths around him.

He married another cook, Nyambura, daughter of Kîboi.

*

My first awareness of Nyambura was when I noticed a woman standing by thingira's porch. For a fleeting moment, the sight confused me. She had pale brown skin and seemed skinnier and taller than Mother. (In 2016, my brother Simon told me I was then three years old.)

Along the way, I overheard someone say my father married another wife. Because I could not conceptualize what a wife meant, I dismissed it as an adult oddity.

Nyambura cooked and lived in thingira because she had no children. But according to custom, the other wife or wives still sent food to the husband. So, Mother continued to send a mug of tea and a dish for Baba. Her only reprieve: she and my brothers did not kindle Baba's fire anymore, and she did not have to provide for his lunch.

In typical polygamous homes, when the food got to thingira, a husband sampled food from each wife. He then chose his favorite dish and offered the rest to his children. To keep the peace, he alternated the dishes he ate. But sometimes things got sticky when a husband seemed to prefer one wife's dishes. Whispers then swirled that so-and-so cooked unpalatable food.

I never heard which food Baba preferred—Nyambura's or Mother's (Kaguyu was out of the picture by then).

But Mother did not concern herself with whose food Baba preferred. She believed no woman cooked Gĩkũyũ food better than she did. Besides, if Baba frowned at her food, which he did not, he would give it to none other than her children.

After Nyambura joined the family, other adjustments followed.

With no way to track Nyambura's movements, the occasional chicken feasts my three brothers enjoyed in the woods ceased forthwith. And violence spiked against my brothers in the name of discipline.

Before Nyambura, Mother reported her boys to my father when she determined they needed discipline from a higher authority. But now, Nyambura did the onus. She reported them for minor infractions like when the goats left for grazing late, or the boys did not answer her if she called them. Based on her reports alone, Baba beat my brothers.

"Keep away from my children," Mother said when she could not stand it anymore. "If you don't, I'll pound you like maize kernels in a mortar, unless you strap yourself to your husband every time he leaves for work."

In her old age, Mother liked to reminisce about such stories. Besides the boys' issue, she claimed Nyambura treated her with disdain as if she, Mother, had no way of fighting back.

I do not doubt Mother itched for an opportunity when she and Nyambura would have a showdown.

Chapter 22

Juggling Two Wives

The Gĩkũyũ saying that *axes in one bag are bound to knock against each other* proved true as soon as Nyambura learned her way around our homestead.

She sent my brothers on errands or ordered them around as if her stepmother status gave her authority over her step-children. Baba confirmed it by punishing the boys based on her reports.

Meanwhile, he managed his household without concern, ignorant of the undercurrent sour relationship that festered between his two wives. He even failed to stick to the true and tried "separate but equal" crafty human control tool and started taking both of his wives to an occasional party. It's likely he wanted to harmonize them away from children and other distractions and, perhaps, show off to his friends.

One Saturday, the three of them attended one of those parties at Gathũmbĩ's homestead. All went well, with an occasional envious glance from a monogamous man or two toward Baba's direction.

On their way home, Baba led through the savanna while his wives followed, jabbering about the party before their exchanges trailed off to family matters.

As Mother claimed later, the amount of alcohol they had drunk had not impaired them, but it had loosened their tongues to tell each other things they would not have dared mention while sober.

Now, their loose mouths fussed about who did what to whom. Halfway home, it escalated to personal insults and attacks.

Finally, to get one up on Mother, Nyambura fired a bazooka.

"You are too old to take care of your husband!" she charged. "That's why he married me!"

"You are a prostitute!" Mother shot back, poking her index finger toward Nyambura. "Probably you are the one who proposed!"

"I'm a wife just like you!" Nyambura said. "My husband married me because he couldn't stand you anymore!"

"You're jealous of my children, you barren prostitute!"

Nyambura rushed at Mother like an American football tackler.

Mother saw her coming, dug in deep, and set herself to receive the blow.

The two flailed their arms, scratched, grabbed, and hurled insults at each other. In the chaos, Nyambura snatched Mother's left thumb, stuck it in her mouth, and her teeth dug in.

"Let go! Let go!" Mother said while she scratched Nyambura's face. Thanks to garden work, Mother's stunted nails traumatized the face but failed to land decent scratches. So, her fingers gravitated toward Nyambura's eyes.

Nyambura let go.

"I'll teach you a lesson!" Mother said. "You'll never attack another woman again!"

The melee continued.

In the tussle, they fell and rolled on the ground.

Baba heard the first part of the quarrel but ignored his bickering *two axes in one bag* and strutted on. He expected them to sort out their differences and catch up with him.

But when he heard a thud, he realized the fight had worsened. He turned around, rushed back, stood about ten feet away, and gawked. His wives wrestled as if each was on a mission to kill the other. Focused on their fight, they paid him no attention.

Baba approached, perhaps expecting them to stop when they sensed his presence.

He got disappointed.

He then forced himself between them and aborted the fight.

Each wife tried to get around him, determined to land one more scratch or fist.

"If you fight again," Baba said, "I'll teach both of you a lesson."

The word of the homestead's ruler called for respect.

The wives moved apart, breathed hard, but restrained their hands.

Baba gazed at them for seconds before he turned and led them home. Not another word passed between the three of them.

They arrived at dusk. Baba and Nyambura headed to thingira while Mother hurried to nyũmba to tend to her children. Before she started, she made a mug of tea for Baba, which he never skipped even when drunk.

His wives' fight must have disturbed Baba a great deal for him to decide to teach them a lesson even though they stopped fighting when he separated and warned them, and no time had elapsed for him to claim they had ignored his warning and fought again.

He, therefore, caught Mother by surprise when he called her to thingira the following morning. After she joined him and Nyambura, he called my brother Simon.

"Bring my whip," he said.

To make the bullwhip supple, he stepped to the porch and cracked it several times before he addressed his wives.

"Because you two craved a fight," he said, "you should fight and get it out of your system."

"Nyacuru, lie down on your stomach," Baba said, and then turned to Nyambura.

"Whip your co-wife five lashes," he said. "After you finish, lie down and she'll do the same to you."

He handed the whip to Nyambura.

"I will not whip anybody," she said, folded her arms and shook her head.

A year into her marriage and Nyambura remained ignorant of the type of man she married, a man who never reconsidered his decisions, no matter how silly, cruel, or unfair.

"All right," Baba said to Nyambura. "Then lie down." He handed the whip to Mother.

She, still bitter that Baba aborted the fight before she "taught Nyambura a lesson," gave Nyambura five lashes with all the energy she could muster. Nyambura twitched after every whip landed but made no other moves.

"Now, give the whip to Nyambura," Baba said.

Mother waited for Nyambura to compose herself and get off the floor.

After she arose, Mother extended the whip to her.

She shook her head, pouted, and crossed her arms yet again.

"Okay," Baba said, "lie down both of you."

He whipped them five lashes each.

"I never want to hear you've assaulted each other again," he said after he finished the count and before he dismissed them

Subsequently, if Baba wanted company, he asked one wife to accompany him at a time.

Mother accompanied him one more time.

"Have you fed the children?" Baba asked her when they returned home.

"I have leftovers," she lied.

There and then, she vowed never to join Baba at a drinking party again. She also stopped drinking alcohol and never touched it again.

Chapter 23

Fruits of Polygamy

Since orphaned as a teenager, Baba had one mission—to grow up, establish a homestead despite the confines of the colony, and continue his family's bloodline. This mission became even more critical when Mwai, his only brother, died in his prime and childless.

Baba's remaining sibling, Aunt Julia, walked out of her marriage as a young woman when her husband married a second wife after she, Aunt Julia, failed to get pregnant.

The only sibling who bore four boys (two of them named Waigwa and Njerũ, after their father's and mother's fathers), was his sister, Wairimũ, buried right there at Kîrîma-inî. But those nephews belonged to a different bloodline, a bloodline Baba cared little about.

His poor sister married a witchcraft peddler by the name of Ndoogo. And when she fell terminally ill, he hauled her all the way from Ragati, Nyeri to Kîrîma-inî and deposited her at Baba's doorstep. He left in haste the following morning, saying he would return soon to check on her.

After two weeks of nursing while she ate little, Aunt Wairimũ became chatty, which gave the family hope she would heal. By mid-day, she said she felt an urge to eat goat meat and insisted her brother get her some.

She and Aunt Julia were the only people who could demand things or talk to Baba as equals, or even throw verbal tantrums.

As Baba and my half-brothers slaughtered a goat, Aunt Wairimũ complained they were taking too long.

Meanwhile, Baba asked someone to get the grill going. As soon as they opened the stomach, he cut out the liver and put it on the grill so his sister could eat and hush while they dismembered the carcass and roasted the meat. When the liver roasted, he cut half of it into bite-size pieces and served it to her.

"It's about time I ate this meat," Aunt Wairimũ said as she propped on elbows on the plank bed where she spent her days and nights.

After she steadied herself, she put one piece in her mouth and chewed several times. When swallowing, she gasped, drew her last breath, and fell back.

Baba and company dug a grave and buried her the same day.

Except hearing of sightings, nobody in Solai saw or heard from her husband again.

*

So far, despite the confines of the farm, Baba had established a semblance of a Gĩkũyũ homestead.

So, when his two wives knocked heads, his homestead structure blinded him. He took time to realize the tension that smoldered within his family since he married Nyambura. Based on his next drastic action, however, he reached a stage when he admitted to himself that he had faltered in his quest to attain his dream of a distinguished Gĩkũyũ elder with many goats, wives, and children, all living in harmony.

It puzzled him that his wives could not get along—one wife had children, and the other did not. They lived in separate houses and shared no kitchen facilities that caused many women's conflicts. What was there to fight about?

I doubt he considered sharing a husband a factor.

Gossip, which must have reached Baba, swirled that Nyambura had become friends with Kaguyu, the divorced first wife, who now lived at Kabati in a house Werũ, the bonus son, had built for her next to his.

According to family members, whenever Nyambura went to her small garden at Kabati, she visited Kaguyu. During those visits, Kaguyu acquainted Nyambura with the family dynamics and how best to ingratiate herself to Baba and become indispensable.

"You are the bride and the favorite wife," Kaguyu told Nyambura, "Nyacuru will have to bow to your wishes."

Other *rumors* surfaced that Nyambura was infertile, the reason Mother threw *thata* (barren woman) at her during their fight and turned her into a thumb chewer. But I doubt Baba cared about that—he had more than enough children.

Or infertility could have been the reason he married Nyambura.

These rumors did not unsettle Mother. She, already a mother of three sons and two daughters, had become too entrenched in the family to feel threatened.

And by the casual manner she told the story later, including the co-wife news, perhaps she even felt relieved to have Nyambura around, if only she could leave her sons alone.

With her hands full to spare much time for fights, Mother threw herself into her part-time job at Kamunge's, her garden, and her children. She produced enough food to go around. Except for the food and tea that she made for Baba, she ran her own household.

But Nyambura sent David and Simon on errands as if they were her children. Although this irritated Mother, it was not the main rub. What irked her the most was that Baba punished the boys when Nyambura reported their lapses.

To minimize accusations, my brothers stayed out of Nyambura's way whenever they could.

But two-year-old Tabitha toddled across the courtyard and entered thingira whenever she chose.

"Give the child something to eat," Baba said when Tabitha stopped by.

"There is nothing left," Nyambura said. Or "I'm busy right now; I'll cook shortly."

"You have nothing in this whole thingira for a child?"

Nyambura would keep quiet.

*

Because Baba never talked about his family, nobody could tell how long he anguished about the dynamics of his polygamous lifestyle and the disharmony it had brought to his homestead.

Two years after Nyambura joined the family, however, he showed how much the tension had bothered him.

He invited his friend Paul and another man early one Sunday—never mind that people did not invite guests in the mornings.

Nyambura made tea for them.

The men made small talk while they drank the tea. As soon as they emptied their mugs, Baba made his intentions known.

"Nyambura," he called out.

"Yes?"

"Go through this thingira and pack whatever belongs to you."

Everyone froze. For seconds, no one said a word.

"Kamwana's father, is there a problem?" Nyambura asked when she composed herself.

(Because David was named after Baba's father, Nyambura called him *lad* as a sign of respect. Daughters and sons-in-law never called their parents-in-law by their names, even the children named after those in-laws.)

"There won't be any debate or discussion," Baba said. "I just want you to pack."

Nyambura froze again; this time for almost a minute.

Tension built up, but no one spoke.

She then started packing.

How much could she pack? Except for her clothes, she owned nothing else besides memories of two years that she needed to process as she walked about.

When she finished, she deposited her wooden box and two small bundles by the threshold and waited for the next order.

"Paul?" Baba said. "Take this woman and hand her over to her uncle, Mũturi. I won't discuss this matter again. I don't even want a refund of my bride price."

The two men exchanged glances. They then got on their feet and left with Nyambura in tow.

*

My father's divorce from Nyambura went contrary to tradition. He summoned the two men to our home and never said, publicly, the reason he sent Nyambura away.

In Gĩkũyũ custom, if a husband could not bear to remain married to his wife, he sent men to return her to her parents. A negotiation ensued to decide whether the husband should get back a portion of the bride price or lose the entire amount.

The representatives started by telling the parents the reasons their daughter's husband decided to divorce her. Reasons included:

- Infertility
- Refusal to render conjugal rights without reason
- Practicing witchcraft
- Becoming a habitual thief
- Willful desertion

- Persistent gross misconduct.

Besides the above reasons, a wife could have divorced her husband because of cruelty, ill-treatment, drunkenness, and impotence.

*

In 2014, I interviewed Gathoni, my then eighty-four-year-old half-sister, and asked her to tell me why Baba divorced Nyambura.

"When Nyambura drank," Gathoni said, "she became unruly like a drunken man."

"What do you mean?"

"One day, she drank and became unhinged," Gathoni said. "Baba and another man took and locked her in thingira's bedroom to calm her. But she climbed over the wall and fell into the sitting area."

"I remember that commotion," I said. "I saw two men pick her from the floor."

"But that wasn't the only reason—"

"There were others?" I asked and bent slightly toward Gathoni, ready to hear a family secret.

"Your mother contributed to Nyambura's marriage break-up?"

"My mother?"

"Yes, she undermined Nyambura's relationship with Baba."

Oh, please. Let Mother rest in peace! I wished I could tell Gathoni.

I suspected she believed her mother's marriage also broke up because of my mother, but I kept that to myself.

I recall two incidents about Baba and Nyambura's marriage. The first one is a blurred awareness of her as she stood by thingira's porch, her hand clasped around the post. The second time was during the commotion when she fell over the wall.

Then she disappeared, and serenity returned to our homestead as if Nyambura never existed.

My memory of her dissipated the following two years we lived at Kîrîma-inî, before our family received orders to move.

Chapter 24

Kîbagio

Polygamy caused rancor in our family because of jealousy and diverse personalities. But most anxieties that unsettled people, and that they could not divorce themselves from, came from unequal laws, containment, and control of Africans by the colonial government and its agents.

Since his youth in Nyeri, Baba had suffered the oppressive laws and poor treatment from officials, the reason he moved away. But now at Kamunge's farm, he felt insulated from colonial troubles. He and his family lived in a secluded homestead tucked away in one corner of the farm, with a footpath as the only outside connection.

His relief, however, lasted until the law reared its head, this time not because of taxation, which Kamunge deducted from his wages with no accounting required, but because of his goats, one *pillar* of his homestead.

In Gîkûyû tradition, the land came first and then goats. Besides barter, the community used goats for currency to settle debts, pay fines and bride prices, amass wealth, and provide milk and meat for the family. It was a sign of respect if a person visited and the host slaughtered a goat.

When the British quashed natives' uprisings and occupied Kenya, they turned it into a protectorate—to protect explorers and missionaries—before they turned the country into a colony. They then passed laws that prohibited what Africans could plant or raise.

One stipulation made it unlawful for Africans to raise billy and nanny goats.

But the British farmers did not enforce that law, at least not in Solai. Even when they noticed, they warned their workers but did not follow through or enforce the prohibition.

But long-term farmworkers like Baba started working for those British farmers when some of them owned little and struggled to pay wages. Focused on establishing themselves, the farmers did scrutinize what their employees did scattered miles apart in the sprawl of farms, most impassable but for the footpaths.

Under the live-and-let-live incidental setup, employees reared the prohibited animals without concern.

They not only liked the look of the elegant, artistic horns but also claimed that, unlike sheep or other variety of goats, billy and nanny goats:
- were more intelligent and easier to herd
- clothes and straps made from their skins were easier to treat, came out softer, and lasted longer
- meats were tastier and leaner because they ate a variety of leaves
- provided milk for their children.

Nanny and billy goats also hardly went astray when their herders got distracted while they climbed trees, constructed toys, practiced target-shooting, terrorized birds with their slingshots, or scavenged for wild fruits. Sometimes a young herder lost the outlawed goats, worried senseless, only to find the herd safely at home.

In contrast, regular goats and sheep grazed on grass or plants closer to the ground, which made their products not as highly prized. People considered them dumber than the outlawed billy and nanny goats.

If their herder slackened on his duty, the regular goats never found their way home.

To help them, especially when they strayed, Baba put bells around the necks of two or three that he considered more intelligent than the rest. These were usually females with kids or a popular male. The kids wore smaller bells so their mothers could locate them easily and not get distracted from their leadership roles.

Goat mothers, like humans, insisted on locating their kids when they romped with others around bushes. No goat agreed to leave for home or lead without her kid beside her.

Baba also branded some goats, mainly the neutral-colored ones with no notable marks, for easier identification if they mixed with other herds.

Even with bells, the regular goats and sheep still became confused when it rained, separated from the leaders, and got themselves lost. This resulted in a search party of men in heavy coats, supplied as their work ration by Kamunge, and boys in raggedy calico shirts.

The searchers walked through the woods half the night and usually found the goats huddled together unless, on a rare occasion, one bumped into a predator.

So, in Solai and Nakuru County, and perhaps all the *White Highlands* (European-only settlements), the peasants preferred the forbidden billy and nanny goats.

It came as a surprise when, in 1945, *Kĩbagio* (indiscriminate "sweeper"), a white inspector with a handful of armed British police with a group of their African subordinates, descended on our homestead at 5:00 in the morning.

To awaken my family, they banged on doors as only the police could. The grownups awoke and opened doors to flashlights on their faces.

"Where do the other goats sleep?" The inspector asked.

(Baba owned so many goats he could not fit all of them indoors).

Baba pointed to the goats' cottage.

The inspector then told him and his family to stand aside. My parents and the older children gawked in horror at the chaos. The gangs rounded the bleating goats, seized them, and loaded them into a procession of monster lorries of that era, which did not need proper roads to get close to our homestead.

They left five goats with orders for Baba to phase them out in two weeks.

Hours later, my family learned that similar raids took place all over the surrounding areas.

With homesteads sprinkled in various parts of farms, however, the authorities lacked the capacity to round up all the animals and carry them in one swoop. By the time Kîbagio reached some homesteads, their owners had already learned of the raid and hidden most of their animals in the woods.

The raiders took thousands of goats to a field in Nakuru town where the colonial administration auctioned them to members of the British settlers' network.

According to my brother Simon, Baba lost about 200 goats.

*

After the sweep, and after the two weeks' grace period, owning a single billy or nanny goat became a hush-hush affair. But Baba still kept a handful of them mixed with the regular herd. He phased them out two or three years after we moved to the village, when it became hard for him to conceal them.

Between ages of eight and ten, I recall three nanny goat slaughters. I can attest that the meat did not have the fat I disliked, and it tasted more delicious than the meats from the regular goats that Baba usually slaughtered.

Because the animals ate leaves, Mother rinsed and strained the contents of the large stomach (abomasum) that looked like half-chewed gobs of green salad. A dark green thick liquid similar to a smoothie remained. She then mixed a measure of it with maize flour and cooked us green porridge that she claimed was medicinal.

With no sugar, the porridge tasted bland and smelled leafy, which my siblings and I hated and tolerated as we did medicine. I waited for the porridge to cool, opened my mouth, rested the rim of the mug on my lip, shut my eyes, and gulped the porridge down, taking one break halfway.

Mother put the rest of the uncooked mixture into a two-gallon size gourd to ferment for future use.

Chapter 25
Goat Pedigree

According to Mother, Baba suffered a great deal when *Kĩbagio* whisked his goats away. But he said nothing during the operation. He stepped aside as ordered, tightened his jaws, and later became listless for about a week.

I now wonder whether it ever occurred to him that he caused similar, if not more, anguish to his family because as the colonialists jerked him, he in turn jerked his family or became outright violent, especially to my brothers.

I know Baba loved his children in his own way, but I'm not sure where he put them in the hierarchy of importance. Without land, honor and goats featured very high to my father.

Anyone in the family who upset his goats expected a bad day—a terrible day indeed.

This happened when herders got distracted and focused too much on their activities. Most times goats grazed, looked after their young, socialized, and waited.

But, occasionally, the animals strayed, became disoriented, and lost themselves in the woods, or helped themselves to people's gardens. This caused ninety percent of my father's violence against my brothers.

I started hearing about the beatings two years after we moved to the village. A year later, at nine, I witnessed how lethal Baba could be to my brothers.

Regarding incidents that took place before my birth, or when I was too young to recall, I include only those accounts I confirmed with victims or eyewitnesses.

*

Despite the seizure of Baba's forbidden goats, he still hid two or three of them in an enclosure in Nyũmba. He also kept a handful of them mixed with the regular herd. This included a pedigree billy goat with massive horns that rivaled those of a buffalo.

Baba's friend, Mũkuhî, envied that billy goat so much that he wanted to own a goat from its bloodline.

The two arranged for Mũkuhî to bring his nanny goat to live among Baba's herd until it bore a pedigree.

At the time, David was away in Nyeri dealing with hunger, and Joseph, at five, had not become a goat herder trainee to accompany Simon to the grasslands. So, contrary to tradition, Baba gave our fourteen-year-old half-sister, Wairimũ-big, a boy's job. He partnered her with nine-year-old Simon.

From the first day, the farmed-in nanny goat rebelled and refused to join the herd. Wairimũ-big and Simon plodded and shooed her until it calmed down and inched closer to the herd. But other times it skipped away, ears perked like a wild animal, and grazed alone.

After two days of pure trouble, the two herders agreed one of them mind the one goat until it got used to the herd.

"A day later, that Saturday," Simon said, recounting the experience after decades, "we rounded the herd to return home."

"The goat got used to the herd?" I asked.

"Are you joking?"

"No," I said.

"The goat behaved like a possessed animal," Simon said. "When either of us rounded that animal, it inched closer to the others, then freaked out and scurried away.

"One time, it stopped about twenty-five feet from where we waited with the herd. It then faced us with crazed, dilated eyes, ears perked. But each time I took a step toward that goat, it skipped and backed off several steps. After three tries, the goat galloped and disappeared into the woods."

"How did you get it back?"

"We looked everywhere," Simon said, "and stopped just before dusk and headed home in case it got too dark and the herd got spooked. We reported the incident to Baba when we arrived."

Besides the two wives and the very young, the entire family went to search for the pedigree. Baba and one of my half-brothers each carried a flashlight. The others carried sticks and followed the person with the flashlight before their eyes adapted.

When people reached where the goat disappeared, they fanned out. They combed the area for hours but found no telltale signs.

Early the next morning, Baba skipped his market day to resume the search with others.

About two hours later, one searcher came to a brushy area.

"Hey! Hey! Come!" he called out to the others.

Strewn about were bloody leftovers of skin and bones.

"It's as if bulls fought here last night!" one searcher said.

Because of the violence involved that flattened the grass and plants, the searchers could not find good paw prints to determine the type of predator.

Baba dismissed the searchers but remained in the woods, perhaps still wondering how to explain the loss of the goat to his friend.

He returned home about half an hour later.

Within five minutes, he called out to Simon and Wairimũ-big.

The two rushed to *thingira*.

They found him by the entrance.

As soon as they entered, Baba closed the door, which revealed a pile of fresh sticks by the wall.

They started to shake.

Baba took a stick from the pile and swung. He swung and swung and swung.

The two herders hollered and apologized.

"We'll never lose another goat again."

"Baba, have mercy on us."

They should have saved their pleas.

When the beating became monotonous, or his right hand got tired, Baba diversified.

Using long leather ropes, he bound each child's hands in front and legs at the ankles, leaving about a foot of rope on each side. He then took the two ends and wrapped them around the center pole. The two herders now lay on their sides on the dirt floor, hogtied around the pole.

Baba got a fresh stick and started another round.

"He beat us on our backs, legs, and arms until it didn't hurt anymore," Simon said.

I had heard from others about their ordeal, but it was not until 2016 that I spoke to Simon about it. He confirmed and gave me a more detailed account.

I interviewed Wairimũ-big a week after Simon. She told me a similar version.

"Baba stopped beating a child only when he became exhausted," Wairimũ-big said, "and couldn't spare extra energy. He hated Simon and me and beat us the most."

Even after sixty years, Wairimũ-big's voice choked, and she had to pause several times. She broke down after the last sentence and could not continue.

Despite Baba's violent bent, my young age shielded me from the abuse my siblings and half-siblings suffered under Baba's hands. So, except for the time he whipped me at age four for potty training, my memory of my family in Kĩrĩma-inĩ is full of contentment.

Later, in the village, my relief came because of my gender—fathers left the discipline of daughters to their mothers. And my mother was not into violence other than a pinch here and a swat there.

And Baba could not recruit me as a temporary goat-herder, the only reason that would have compelled him to cross the gender line and assault me. I already held a full-time babysitting job.

Chapter 26

Wacky Discipline

While goats caused about ninety percent of the violence in my family, the other ten percent came from childhood transgressions and crimes.

The chicken theft fell under this category, but Nyambura breezed into our courtyard before Baba caught up with my brothers.

The other children's crime Baba considered as bad, if not worse, came about because we did not grow fruits. Like the billy and nanny goats, the colonial administration prohibited Africans from growing perennials or cash crops. The officials did not give their reasons.

But people knew—from gossip that trickled down to the village—that if they grew unlawful crops, especially cash crops, it would dilute the British farmers' monopoly on trade.

Besides, the crops would have provided better nutrition for the African families, and they would have earned extra income to take their children to school. Most parents could not afford school fees.

The income would have also given Africans something to fall back on when they lost their jobs.

To the colonizers, however, Africans needed to remain satisfied as dependents with no permanent homesteads outside the cramped native reserve. Missionaries and their now trained and indoctrinated African surrogates reminded them often that this world was not their home. Their home awaited them in heaven, where they would find opulence laid out, with no more suffering or dying.

Meanwhile, permanence, self-determination, and freedom came with ownership, and the luxury of ownership belonged to the British landowners who grew whatever they chose.

Fruits fell into the perennial category.

To ensure no employee planted a perennial plant behind his back, every year before planting season, Kamunge sent his tractor driver to plow the plots he allocated to his male employees.

(He did this after the tractor finished plowing his plantations, the reason Mother complained before she stole Kamunge's maize.)

So, on Kamunge's farm, like other European farms, fruits grew either in the wild or at his orchard.

Older children scavenged for certain fruits in the woods when they walked from school or took goats to pasture. Little children and their parents ate no fruits. And parents warned their children with severe beatings and jail term (this had already happened) if they ventured close to Kamunge's orchard.

But which parent could guarantee his or her child would not fall into temptation?

I doubt it crossed my parents' minds that my brothers could get tempted, or even that they knew an orchard existed.

But David, at thirteen, and Simon, at eleven, knew of the orchard. And they fell into temptation.

When the two went goat herding, they banded with other boys and walked east for at least four miles to Kamunge's orchard. They approached from behind, sneaked in through the barbed wires, and stole oranges. After they ate their fill, they hid the rest for the following day.

Late afternoon, they headed home with a well-fed herd of goats.

Baba joined them and the three of them shooed and corralled the goats into their cottage. When Baba and David secured the gate, Simon checked and secured the chicken coop. Animals safe for the night, Baba returned to thingira where he now lived alone since he ran off Nyambura.

David and Simon sighed with relief as their fear vanished. It had gripped them when Baba came to help corral the goats. Their fear spiked whenever he came close, as if he could read their minds.

But Baba, with his keen vulture-like nose, didn't need to read any boy's mind.

They now went to nyũmba, a father-free sanctuary, and sat by the fire to wait for supper, believing their crime behind them.

In Gĩkũyũ custom, a man never entered his wife's house except after their children became adults, left the house, and established their own households, or in an emergency.

Now, an emergency befell Baba's homestead.

He appeared at nyũmba's threshold.

In a split second, the boys scattered.

Simon dashed into Mother's bedroom and stood squeezed in a corner, close to some hanging clothes.

Baba rushed after him into the pitch-dark room and felt the walls, corners, and hung clothes.

At one time, he touched Simon's shirt. Simon held his breath and stilled his body. Baba mistook the shirt for the hanging clothes and moved on. But unfamiliar with Mother's bedroom, he groped around and tripped on things. He soon gave up and headed back to the living area.

Simon's mind went into overdrive. He recalled what happened to him and Wairimũ-big because of the pedigree goat. He feared a similar fate awaited him.

How long could he remain hidden? Not long. Mother would soon light her lantern when darkness eased in.

Distracted by developments in the living area, Simon suspended his worries and listened.

From my parents' exchanges, he learned David had clambered up like a monkey and hid where humans did not dare step in. He put up with the heat and the smoke, determined to wait it out, perhaps believing our parents sane enough not to follow him up there.

Soon, Baba returned to the living area.

"David went up in *Itara*" (the firewood storage bed over the fire pit), Mother said.

Baba went outside and armed himself with an armful of pieces of firewood from the pile Mother kept under the eaves near the porch.

Back inside, he put the pile on the floor and threw one piece at a time onto the *itara*.

Mother stood by and watched.

David choked from the heat and smoke, but the firewood assault overwhelmed him.

He jumped down the seven feet and landed in a heap by the door.

Before he recovered to scuttle through the exit, Baba grabbed his shirt. Instead of first checking whether his son suffered broken bones as a normal father would do, Baba started his assault.

He slammed, slapped, roughed, and beat his thirteen-year-old as if the two were in a no-rules wrestling match.

At the height of Baba's insanity, Simon shot out of the bedroom like an arrow. Mother, standing by like a referee, got spooked and yelped when he ran into her and almost knocked her to the floor.

As soon as Simon cleared the threshold, he rounded the house to the back, stood under the eaves, and perked his ears.

As the beating intensified, David's body went into survival mode. He stopped crying, screaming, or trying to get away. He lay there and took the blows.

"Baba, you're beating me as if I'm a grown man you are fighting with," David said, a line Mother and others later repeated many times.

"On hearing this," Simon told me, "I cried."

After fifty-seven years, Simon still choked up as he told me that story. David's beating must have affected him more because he never choked when he told me about his own beating during the pedigree goat incident.

Mother told us the orange assault story in my teen years, and, again, in my adulthood. She blamed Baba for having gone too far in his punishments. My siblings and I never let her know we knew she told on David.

To her credit, Mother never reported my brothers to Baba again. Instead, she dealt with their infractions on her own, with a whack here and a pinch there, but mainly with her vocal mouth.

None of us wanted to hear her loud mouth, especially when we moved to the village, and she did not mind who heard her reprimand us.

She also never threatened with, "Wait until your father comes home," a warning I later heard many abused and powerless mothers use.

State

of

Emergency

Chapter 27

The Exodus

The freedom I enjoyed that built fond memories while I accompanied my mother to her job or our garden lasted only six months before our lives changed.

Mother talked about an emergency. I heard my grandmother Nyandia say the same word four months earlier when she came to see baby Morry.

What did it mean? I noticed no changes in our family.

I later learned men known as Mau Mau had rebelled against the colonial government and taken to the forest to fight for the return of their seized lands and independence. To calm European settlers' jitters and to *protect* them from the peasant Gĩkũyũ population—and Mau Mau members, in particular—the colonial Governor, Sir Evelyn Baring, declared a state of emergency in the entire country on October 21, 1952.

The previous day, the government had arrested Jomo Kenyatta and a group of 129 Gĩkũyũ political activists that included a handful of non-Gĩkũyũ supporters.

The authorities never told the men where they were taking them until the so-called dissidents arrived at the Kapenguria Detention Camp in arid Northern Kenya. That became their torture and hard-labor center for the next seven years.

Then the colonial government ordered the rest of Gĩkũyũ tribe—men, women, and children—to move to *secure* villages on farms or in *native reserves*. The government sent to concentration camps the ones they accused or claimed supported or affiliated with the Mau Mau.

The first thing I noticed was noisy activities by a family behind our homestead. I have forgotten whatever prior association I may have had with them.

"The lorry is here!" A man shouted and others echoed. "The lorry has arrived!"

I heard rumbling noises, perhaps my first vehicle sound ever, but I could not yet see what they referred to.

A man and woman and their friends dashed behind our homestead. They reappeared carrying baskets and two small wooden suitcases. A woman held a crying child in her arms while she hustled two others, one my age and the other smaller.

I later learned that was my half-brother's family— Waigwa and his wife, Njeri, with their six-year-old daughter, Mũmbi; four-year-old son, Mũthee, and two-year-old daughter, Wambũi.

The ruckus grew robust when the lorry, already full of people, stopped a short distance behind Baba's thingira.

Nobody took things from nyũmba, which made me conclude my family was not riding in that lorry. Curious, I inched closer. Others did the same, but I paid them no attention; it seemed like too much confusion.

Two men from the lorry got off to help Waigwa's family board. They squeezed in with whatever few belongings they carried.

Waigwa's mother, Kaguyu, his sister Wairimũ-big and Njoroge, her new husband, were already on board, having got on the lorry at Kabati where they had been living with Werũ, the bonus son.

People complained that *mzungu* aka Kamunge should have arranged for two lorries for the area. Women stood at the center of the lorry's bed, others sat on their luggage to protect it from hurried or careless feet. Some mothers hushed their screaming babies held to their chests with ngoi and cloth sheets, others comforted children on their laps or beside them.

Men lined the periphery, some in old work trousers under untucked shirts and some like Waigwa wore hats, their sandaled right feet firmly on the lorry's edge, hands tightened around sidebars of the canopy-less lorry.

The lorry took off like a getaway car before passengers settled in. A hat flew off one man's head. He flailed his arms to catch it, but he stopped when another man asked him whether he wanted to fly away like his hat.

Lorries made several trips along Solai Road to haul people who waited in designated spots.

Werũ and his bride, Ruth, Alan's daughter, planned to take a later ride. Not long married, the couple had no children to worry about and traveled light.

At a distance from where they waited by the roadside, they saw Alan hurrying toward them, arms swinging, an unusual behavior given his mild nature.

"That's my father," Ruth said. "I hope nothing is wrong."

"We'll know soon enough," Werũ replied.

By the time Alan reached them, he breathed heavily and spared no energy for explanations.

"Take your luggage and head home right now," he said to his daughter, thrusting his index finger toward her and then homeward.

"I leave my husband?" Ruth asked, eyes wide, perplexed.

"You aren't going to that native reserve!"

Ruth pouted and fought off tears.

Werũ became stupefied.

"Now!"

Ruth picked up her small wooden suitcase and turned her back on her husband, likely hoping she could smuggle herself on a later ride.

Werũ went to the roadside a married man but rode on the lorry wife-less and depressed, a minor hiccup compared to the turmoil that would choke the country for years.

Kaguyu's other two children did not join in the exodus. Gathoni, the second daughter, remained with her husband and child in Subukia area six miles away, where she still lives today.

The youngest son, Gĩthũi-big, left with Aunt Julia and her boyfriend, Ishmael Gĩcũhĩ, in 1945. He lived at Mr. Gĩcũhĩ's home in Mũrang'a County, where he attended elementary and middle schools.

Except for their mother, Kaguyu, none of the family members who traveled by lorry had ever visited their destination, the so-called Native Reserve.

In my teens, I learned that during the exodus Kamunge, like the other European farmers, handpicked the employees who would remain on the farm. He included my half-brother Waigwa. A man of calm disposition, Kamunge liked him because he followed rules and required no supervision.

To remain on the farm, however, an employee had to put a thumbprint (*gũtheca kĩrore*) because most people did not know how to write. This meant signing a loyalty agreement that stated no matter the results of the Mau Mau uprising, the employee would remain loyal and defend the farm.

Waigwa and his half-brother, Werũ, refused to sign. Kamunge enticed Waigwa, offering him the overseer job when Baba retired, which nobody knew when but many years into the future. Kamunge also promised he would protect loyal employees against harassment by the colonial government and by the Mau Mau.

Waigwa remained adamant and insisted on leaving.

Kamunge asked Baba to intervene.

Baba happily did; he preferred his son to remain as well. Except for Mother, a woman, Waigwa remained the only grown relative that Baba could count on.

"Are you sure you want to go?" Baba asked Waigwa.

"Yes, I cannot sign those papers."

"Weigh the matter carefully," Baba said. "There is too much turmoil going on."

"I don't want to remain tied to Kamunge like a wife to a husband."

Waigwa, like his brother Werũ, bet on a Mau Mau win. The idea and prospect of independence and people getting their lands back from the British intoxicated them.

Besides, they had a head start because their oldest brother, Njerũ-big, and sister, Wanjirũ-big, and their spouses already lived in Nyeri, where they moved several years before the war broke out.

I believe Baba felt relieved after Kaguyu, his ex-wife, boarded that lorry. There is a Gĩkũyũ saying that says *ũtumia wĩ mwana ndateagwo* (a wife with a child is never divorced). If she stayed in Solai, despite the divorce, people would still have referred to her as Warama's wife.

So, Baba welcomed the added distance. Besides, by the exodus, he had enough of polygamy and had settled with Mother, and I doubt he wanted to meddle with that stability.

I also doubt Mother sacrificed a tear to see Kaguyu leave. She strutted in our courtyard as if she were the first wife and needed no reminder that she came in second after Kaguyu.

Kaguyu could not have minded, either. After a stormy and broken thirty-year marriage, she preferred to return to Nyeri among her people, where she was born and raised.

We—Baba's second family—remained behind because he swore when he left Nyeri that, war or peace, his family would never return to Nyeri if he had any say.

Still, our lives changed.

Chapter 28

Kabati

Not more than a week after the exodus lorry left, I heard Mother say Kamunge did not want his employees scattered all over the farm. He wanted them where he could keep an eye on them, to protect them from the alleged Mau Mau "terrorists."

I did not know that included my family until the commotion I saw during the lorry ride started in our homestead.

I then understood why Baba arrived home at dusk the previous week or two. As I learned later, he was building another place for us to move. But the only part I recall was when he and two men dismantled our granary and carried big posts on their shoulders.

Mother packed and carried on her back piles and piles of our household effects. It took her several days to finish. Tabitha and I, at six and four, were too young to help her with female chores. But I may have helped carry baby Morry on our last day at Kîrîma-inî; I'm not sure.

We moved to Kabati about three miles away.

When we arrived, the cottages' muddy walls were still damp and the fresh grass-thatch still with streaks of green. Women finished the thatch on one of the two hovels on the day we arrived. The two cottages resembled a campsite in the middle of the savanna, with no inside partitions.

My memory is stuck on Mother seated on a low bench on one side of the fire pit, Morry in her lap while she complained about the hurried move, the lack of room for the family and animals, and the-not-fit-for-human shack.

"This dampness will make my children catch pneumonia," she said. Another time I heard her say, "The dampness will kill my children."

She especially worried about the youngest ones, Morry at six months and Gîthũi at two-and-a-half years old.

The one thing Mother did not complain about was the fireplace. The three masonry stones, which she must have scavenged at the quarry, looked sturdier and newer. They could support a sizeable pot without stress of tipping over.

Besides the moving activity, Mother fetched food, cooked, and cared for her family. By the time she left work or the garden, baby Morry on her back or front, arrived home and kindled the fire, it was late afternoon.

Saddled with an infant while her hungry brood's little eyes focused on her, Mother hurried to cook supper. She worked from dawn until bedtime. But she took it in stride because, according to her, *njogu ndîremagwo nî mîguongo yayo* (an elephant is never defeated by its tusks).

But one day, one of her tusks rattled her when pressure peaked and caused her to suffer a second's worth of insanity and turn into a crazed fire thrower.

It started with the death of a chicken when Mother arrived home one late Saturday afternoon. She boiled a big pot of water and told my older brothers—David, Simon, and Joseph—to catch a certain chicken for slaughter, no doubt after she sought permission from Baba.

My brothers cherished that kind of task because not only were they going to eat a delicacy but also because they enjoyed chases, especially sanctioned ones. Baba in his thingira—well, in his temporary shack then—would not click his tongue and ask, "What's that racket all about?"

So, my brothers dashed this way and that amidst their shrieks and screams while the terrified chicken squawked and flapped its wings until it ran out of options.

When one of them handed the chicken to Mother, she subdued it by clasping its wings at the shoulders with her left hand like handcuffs. With her right, she held its legs along with a knife she had sharpened on a file Baba kept in his thingira.

The poor chicken squawked and squawked as Mother marched behind the cottage. Curious and eager to witness our first slaughter, Tabitha and I followed at a distance, while Gĩthũi toddled behind us.

Mother laid the chicken on its side in a grassy area. She stepped on its wings with her left foot and on the legs with her right. She then held the head and clapped the beak to stop the cries, and raised her right arm, knife in hand. We caused a rustle. She turned toward the house and saw us.

"Go back to your play," she said.

We trotted back to the front.

Within no time, Mother emerged dangling the chicken by its legs, head halfway cut, blood still oozing from the neck wound with an occasional drip.

In all my six years, I had not witnessed a single slaughter, but that day, I connected our meat and its source. Subsequently, whenever Mother or Baba slaughtered a hen or a goat, they did so out of our sight. If we rushed to see, they shooed us away as if they did not want us to witness them kill an animal.

In the house, Mother removed the pot of boiling water from the fire. She dunked the chicken into the hot water, then held the legs and rolled the chicken from one side to the other. The pauses between the rolls loosened the feathers without peeling the skin. Whenever she turned the chicken, a gush of hot steam flared and assaulted our little faces.

"Stand back!" Mother said. "This can burn you."

We stood back, wiped moisture from our faces, and claimed we could handle it before we closed in to gawk again.

Mother scooped hot water with a white mug and poured it over the knees that she could not submerge. When she determined the feathers loose enough, she pulled the chicken out and rested it on a tin basin.

After the chicken cooled somewhat, my brothers helped pluck it. They pulled fistfuls of feathers and finally picked out the tiniest feathers around the knees and the neck.

Mother then turned the carcass over a flame to zap the tiny pin-hairs fingers could not grab and pluck.

To cut the chicken, she opened the stomach, removed the intestines and the stomach, and put them aside for the cat. She discarded the head and the feet, parts we later learned in the village that some people ate.

Mother sautéed green leafy onions in oil and browned the chunks. She added salt before she added enough water into the pot to cook. She also put fresh firewood into the fire from each of the fire pit's three sides.

Whoever held baby Morry, most likely David or Simon, handed him back to Mother after she settled back in her seat. She put him in her lap. The rest of us children huddled around the other two sides of the fire.

"Don't get too close to the fire," Mother said. "I don't want to end up with a scorched child."

We talked, watched, and waited in anticipation for the chicken to cook.

Meanwhile, Simon had claimed the chicken's stomach as he, David, and Joseph did whenever Mother slaughtered a chicken. Because darkness had set in, he cleaned it indoors and made himself a balloon.

He now stood at one side of the cottage and blew into the balloon. Whenever he let go, the air escape caused the balloon to snap and sail overhead clear across the room. In one instance, however, instead of flying, the balloon smacked POW! right into the bubbling soup.

Hot splashes and droplets sprayed in every direction.

David and Joseph howled and shot to their feet.

We little children fell back, Tabitha or Gîthũi ended up on the floor. We shrieked and cried while we wiped our faces and finally got on our feet.

Mother half spun away from the fire to shield Morry. The second droplets stopped flying, she spun back toward the fire.

"He will burn my children!" she said and simultaneously whipped out a piece of one of the blazing firewood and hurled it at Simon.

He ducked.

The wood missed him by inches.

It hit the wall with a thud, scattered hundreds of sparks that enveloped him, and almost set his shirt ablaze.

Mother's reaction clamped every mouth and sound in the room except for the crackling fire and the bubbling soup.

Even when we settled back, we controlled our usual racket as we waited for food.

When we smacked our mouths in quiet that night, Mother, like me, sneaked glances at Simon. She did not ask him to hold the baby or help with anything else that evening.

Besides Mother's complaints about dampness, the chicken incident remains my only clear incident at Kabati.

After just four months, another commotion descended on our temporary camp. Mother started packing again and making bales of deliveries on her back.

Mũthũngũ nîarericũkirwo (the European changed his mind), she said.

Kamunge, the European, ordered my family to move yet again.

Chapter 29
The Village

We moved into a village at a higher elevation four miles east of Kabati. It contained about a hundred mud and thatch circular houses, most of them in clusters around small courtyards.

A close-knit chain-link fence, of about nine to ten feet high, reinforced by long posts and barbed wire, similar to a prison's, surrounded the village. Several rows of slanting barbed wire crowned the top. We left or entered the village only through a single entrance to the east.

As I learned a year later, another mile eastward lived Kamunge and his family in a sprawl of a farmhouse set in about ten acres. A two-acre orchard—that David and Simon had visited and David paid dearly for—snuggled in a lush shrubbery area that bordered Jumatatu Mountain range to the east and Tindaress River to the south.

Although our adopted homestead was smaller, it looked similar to our previous one at Kîrîma-inî, except it had no goats' cottage. Baba built one with the help of others soon after.

Just like Kîrîma-inî, the homestead faced northwest, and thingira—its back to the village—commanded the best view of the courtyard.

We entered from the side, between thingira and nyũmba. We could see a person enter the courtyard only from the goats' cottage or the granary. Otherwise, we got alerted when a person reached the threshold.

Except children, however, adults did not sneak in on us. Right from the entrance, they cleared their throats, faked a cough, or asked whether anyone was home.

My parents may or may not have known until we arrived at the village that, after the colonial governor declared a state of emergency, Kamunge wanted us out of our secluded home at Kîrîma-inî without further delay. And he intended for us to stay at Kabati only until he got the village fenced and the last shipment of people to the native reserve to vacate the village.

When we arrived, goats and chickens loitered about with no one to restrict their movement, until evening came and each animal gravitated toward its regular homestead. And personal effects remained intact in the houses.

In nyũmba, the house Mother adopted, besides the household items, we found pots, pans, and trays full of roasted goat meat and other cooked foods. More food filled kîondo baskets.

The families who moved into other abandoned homesteads adopted the animals and ate whatever food they found. For the first and last time, women enjoyed cook-free days before they prepared meals for their families.

But no such luck for my mother.

Baba, always the law-abiding colonized, viewed with disdain everything people left behind as if it were tainted or taboo. He forbade my family from eating the food or using the items.

Instead, he and my brothers dug a big hole close to the fence, which he ordered Mother and my brothers to dump in the meat and the other food. He and the boys covered the grave as one would for the dead.

Baba let the animals spend the night. But the next day, he rounded the goats and chickens and gathered the household effects with the help of my brothers and a handful of men. They delivered them to Kamunge's huge storage barn by the colonial farmhouse that housed the farm machinery, odds and ends, and sacks of maize, wheat, and coffee beans before shipment.

I never learned what Kamunge did with the belongings. But it is safe to assume he sold the animals and told his workers to destroy the personal effects, which I suspect they instead kept for themselves.

The two cats we found needed nobody's help. They turned feral and lived free ever after. Well, not really. In time, in need of a family of their own, they gingerly trailed back in and became part of our household.

Except for blurs, I remember very little of this part of the story. At six and a half years old, my only focus and comfort, amidst the uncertainty and all the changes, was my mother's presence.

For clarity, I relied on the stories my family shared as I grew older.

But so many houses clustered together fascinated me, but I was thankful I could play with the children who lived there.

My three older brothers, however, noticed the most enticing display of food they had ever seen or would see in all their formative years. They never forgot a single detail well into their senior years.

Back then, even our mother marveled at Baba's actions.

"How could he be against waste," she asked, "and then turn around and demand such wastage?"

But no one dared question the Great One.

It now puzzles me that Mother did not leave some of the food in her house. Stuck in his thingira, Baba would not have suspected or found out. But that's the state of conditioned minds.

As regards the fence, adults did not have to watch or warn their children about it. Even adventurous Joseph, who embraced life in full, ignored the fence. I doubt he could have scaled a fence with that close-knit barbed wire. Even if he did, he would have fallen into a ditch several feet deep along the outside.

The ditch, like a castle moat, ensured no person braved the fence and entered or left the village other than through the guarded gate—by a non-Gĩkũyũ—to the east.

While my family adjusted to village life, and I grew older, I overhead subdued conversations about the Mau

Mau uprising. Mother said people feared an informant would overhear them. If the information got to Kamunge, he could have labeled the talkers Mau Mau sympathizers, which meant a police interrogation and a likely ride to the feared concentration camps, a place a detainee never knew whether he or she would ever come out alive or not.

I did not bother to eavesdrop on what Baba said. He never indulged in useless talk.

But from the bits of what I heard, I figured Mau Mau members were outlaws who wanted to ruin our lives. For this reason, Kamunge moved and confined us in a camp-like village for our own safety.

My parents and other villagers may have understood Mau Mau's aspirations. But the thought of expelling the British and getting their lands and freedom back seemed insurmountable. It bordered on a community in a tug-of-war with a god.

The oppression they had undergone their entire lives had wiped ideas of ownership and self-determination from their minds. They did not see themselves in any other way except as Kamunge's laborers and subjects, the inheritance that, at a cellular level, they passed on to their children.

So, the villagers did not question when Kamunge ordered a mandatory interrogation for all Gĩkũyũ adults. They got confused, however, because they had already signed the loyalty agreement that they would remain beholden to the farm regardless of the war results. But now the government wanted to interrogate them like criminals?

Kamunge knew they were loyal; why then, they wondered, did he not get them exempted?

But they had no option except to hunker down and follow orders. That remained their motto: keep heads down and raise their children.

At least, I know Baba stuck to a flawless work ethic and never wanted Kamunge to question his loyalty. He would have done anything to ensure nothing made Kamunge and his family uneasy, uncomfortable, or angry.

According to Mother, as the overseer, Baba expected Kamunge would exempt him from the interrogation.

Perhaps his memory of a troubled life under the colonial government as a young man, and the reason that made him abandon Gîkûyûland, had faded from his memory.

Whatever the case, Baba underestimated the determination and power of the British crown and the gravity of the state of emergency.

*

Gradually, I learned that the colonial government segregated Agîkûyû from other tribes so those tribes would not get enticed to join the Mau Mau uprising.

Along the way, I heard people mention the various names European farmers called Africans "natives, primitives, savages, barbarians, monkeys, or bloody Africans."

From women's talk, I learned or sensed that no matter how loyal and hard the Africans worked, Kamunge and other Europeans still viewed them as despicable human beings.

What pathology would make powerful people in charge to treat so poorly those who worked so hard for them—including raising their children, cooking and cleaning for them, and making their beds, and whom they also considered inferior?

My young mind could not figure that out, not even in adulthood.

With the Mau Mau uprising, the colonialists' major thrust was to subdue the Africans, particularly the Gīkūyū tribe, and erase from their minds any lofty ideas about freedom, restoration of their lands, and civil rights.

(Meru and Embu tribes and Tharaka, smaller tribes and close cousins of the Gīkūyū, got sucked into the Mau Mau uprising. This book, however, is a family memoir that focuses on the Gīkūyū farmworkers and Gīkūyūland, the epicenter of the Mau Mau activities.)

Meanwhile, as so-called *primitives* weathered the oppression and indoctrination, they needed to understand that the poor state they found themselves in proved British superiority.

Their masters impressed on these peasants that the militant Gīkūyū men and women, who questioned, challenged, and took to the forests to fight for the rights of their community, were terrorists to be knifed, shot on sight, or bombed.

The bits and pieces I heard about the Mau Mau, amidst our hurried moves and at the village, sounded too complicated for me. But I knew for sure that Kamunge wielded the ultimate power.

But that did not bother me because nothing bad happened to me at our homestead.

And wherever we moved, I believed, my parents were in charge and would ensure my safety, until that became doubtful as well.

Chapter 30

Interrogation

Disruption became a part of our lives since our first move from Kîrîma-inî in early 1953.

Now, in our third residence in less than a year, my mother talked in haste, rushing to do chores. As for Baba, he did not drink or sit on his three-legged stool at the porch to admire his animals anymore.

I was oblivious to what happened in the village then, but through my parents' behavior, it seemed as if the entire village kept busy and alert.

My parents' busyness never concerned me though; our household mornings and evenings rhythms remained the same day-in-day-out.

I also liked that Baba constructed, well, wove, a permanent cot-like bed with high sides, so Tabitha and I would not fall off. It separated Mother's bedroom from the living area, and my sister and I shared an entryway with her. One side made one wall of Mother's bedroom.

The bed's entrance was about two feet high and, for a period, before we got the hang of it, Mother helped us climb in.

Every morning when I awoke, I found her by the fireplace cooking tea, porridge, or getting lunch ready for Baba to carry to work.

And Baba caused his own racket in the courtyard. He puttered around before or after his mug of tea and woke my brothers when they overslept. He also let out goats from their cottage, who then bleated, romped, and caused most outdoor activity before their herder led them to pasture.

One morning, however, I awoke and sensed in minutes that our homestead rhythms had changed. Mother still busied herself with her morning routine, but I heard no activity in the courtyard. Baba would never let goats remain locked up in daylight.

"Where is Baba?" I asked.

"He'll be back soon," Mother said.

"Where did he go?" my younger siblings and I wanted to know.

"*Kũhũngwo mahũri*," (to get interrogated).

"What is interrogated?"

"It's how the government catches wrongdoers."

"Is Baba a wrongdoer?

"Oh! No! It's just a formality."

Mother's explanation of Baba's departure pacified me for a day. But when he did not come home that evening, it looked odd.

Up to that point, my father had always come home after work and never after dark.

That evening, Mother cooked in *thingira* while we huddled around the fire, seated on the floor, or on low benches, subdued.

As days stretched to two, three, and more, malaise descended on us.

Based on our visceral fear of Baba, one would think we would want him gone so we could play with abandon. But, instead, we missed his presence, and we did not play as boisterously as before.

*

We soon learned the colonial government had set interrogation sites all over Gĩkũyũland—Nyeri, Mũrang'a, and Kĩambuu—and on European farms in the Rift Valley and in towns' neighborhoods where Gĩkũyũ people lived.

The site for our area was at Lambert's farm in neighboring Subukia, about eight miles from our village.

Every week, Kamunge selected about eight individuals, and later in the evening, after the village slept, the police sneaked in and hauled them away.

*

Baba endured the "formality" for about eight days. I learned of his return when Mother took him a mug of tea one early morning. He ignored his goats and other activities, and stayed home—the only time I saw him stay home from work.

He remained in his thingira for three days.

After Mother sniffed around for news, she learned that Baba suffered a "higher level" of interrogation than necessary because "Your father is very stubborn," she said.

The report also said, no matter the amount of punishment, he insisted he had not taken the oath. The authorities finally let him go.

News of Baba's torture threw me off.

If he was not a wrongdoer, as Mother said, why did the government punish him?

I questioned Mother's statement of "only a formality."

Before that, my overhearing adult conversation was incidental. But after I realized Mother was not forthcoming, I eavesdropped and hung around adults who dropped by our homestead any chance I got.

I learned detainees suffered increased level of abuse or torture depending on whether the interrogators deemed them innocent, oath-takers, or involved with the Mau Mau.

Torture methods ranged from insults, shoves, slaps to whippings. Also, men suspected of Mau Mau affiliations suffered sleep deprivation, solitary confinement, and private parts torture until they confessed.

Interrogators applied these so-called "milder" methods of torture to Agĩkũyũ left on European farms. The majority who lived or moved to the native reserves, or confined into detention camps, would later report the horrors they endured that included permanent disabilities of mind, limbs, castrations, and deaths.

*

Mother left for the screening camp two weeks after Baba returned to work. Although we did not know when she would leave, she had prepared us.

She said not to worry if we woke one morning and found her gone because "I won't be gone for long."

But that did not pacify me when I woke up and, while I rubbed my eyes to see better, I noticed my brother Simon, at thirteen, stirring porridge, seated on Mother's usual spot. A whiff of panic stabbed me and my world shattered. I had never woken in the morning and not found my mother busy with her chores.

What would I do without her? Everything about my life revolved around my mother, from when I woke up and found breakfast ready to when she cooked supper, while my siblings and I waited around the fire.

Mother's best friend, Wanjeri, came to mother us while Simon picked up the slack.

She cooked or fetched water for us as if we were her own family, but that did not prevent me from experiencing bouts of sadness.

A stub of sadness hit me from time to time and got worse as evening approached. We did whatever Simon asked of us, but we moved slowly, acted subdued and out of sorts.

Wanjeri left early to cook supper for her own children, Baba holed up in his thingira to await whatever food Simon and Wanjeri prepared for him. Meanwhile, the inside of my little chest contracted with occasional agony.

I kept asking myself what would happen to me if Mother never returned. I could not think of an answer besides emptiness.

At almost seven, I was like the little birds huddled in a nest waiting for their mother to return and dump food down their throats.

I became so involved with my plight that I do not recall a single incident with my younger siblings during our mother's absence.

For the first time, I felt helplessness caused by an invisible external power—more powerful than my father.

My anguish because of Mother's absence, however, did not mean I cared less for Baba. I had felt apprehension when he left, but Mother assured us. I also believed that, as a man, nothing could prevent my father from returning home.

But Mother's absence hurt in different ways. Our home seemed and felt empty—the vacuum I agonized about the most.

After Wanjeri left in the evening, Simon, at only thirteen years old, dealt with five children all younger than him, including Morry, still a baby at about one-year-old.

To stress me even more, I overheard grownups talk of beatings. It sounded terrible, which made me wonder whether government officials were beating my mother. Besides the confusion, I did not understand what that meant. I had forgotten my one and only spanking at four, and I had yet to witness another beating.

Baba was no help. He stuck in his thingira ignorant of how to ease our fears, or explain, or talk about the interrogation, then or ever.

His attitude remained firm; he had fulfilled his duty, and nothing would change whether he talked or complained.

In his defense, however, I now doubt he knew we, his children, felt troubled, or that we had overheard as much as we had.

Chapter 31

Screening Camp

Mother returned from interrogation eager to talk. She shared with us children brief episodes but reserved long accounts for her friends. Unlike other times, though, she did not shoo me or any other eavesdroppers away.

I sat nearby whenever a friend came by. It took me a long time to pin the story together because Mother discouraged long social calls. They wasted too much time, she said.

In time, however, enough pieces fell into place that later became clearer when Mother rehashed her camp experience.

At Lambert's camp, she said, the authorities sorted her group by gender. They then hustled each detainee into a dark cottage occupied by others from different farms who she did not know.

Mother ended up in a mud-walled, grass-thatched circular hovel. She found the women occupants leaning against the wall or sitting on the dirt floor. They jabbered about the state of emergency and the best way to endure the camp.

Mother felt her way around in the dark for a free spot to position herself. Not one to dillydally, she could not settle fast enough to join in the conversation.

In case she needed to relieve herself, a woman next to her gave her directions to a lonely tin pail by one side of the un-partitioned cottage.

"Relieve myself in front of people?"

"Well, it's not like we can see you."

Some women must have already helped themselves to the pail because an awful smell engulfed them. That had to be part of the screening hardships, Mother said later.

Before she left home, she had learned through word of mouth that the colonial government declared the state of emergency because the Mau Mau fighters demanded the return of their lands.

She and her friends spoke of how those demands had made their lives harder. They now lived in so-called *secure villages,* subjected to dusk to dawn curfew, forced to rush to work and to their gardens. Kamunge's animals, wandering in a mile or two long and wide pens, enjoyed more freedom of movement than the villagers did.

But now at the camp, detainees exchanged stories and helped Mother connect the political fragments she had gathered. The women who had taken the oath said Mau Mau members were freedom fighters led by Dedan Kimathi, who were fighting the British so they would return the lands they seized from the natives and for Kenya's independence from Britain.

Detainees talked about Jomo Kenyatta's contribution and his alleged association with the Mau Mau. He and his colleagues languished in detention at Kapenguria in Northern Kenya.

But the women in the know, Mother said, disagreed that Kenyatta collaborated with the Mau Mau.

They explained to their colleagues that the Mau Mau were patriots who became weary, waiting for educated activists like Kenyatta to show positive results of their years of campaigns and negotiations with the British about independence and restoration of the seized lands.

Mother wondered how the Mau Mau would accomplish such a monumental task. She grew up on a European farm in Nanyuki, having left Gĩkũyũland as a young girl. Peasant life on a colonial farm was all she knew. Without education to help her understand the intricacies of such possibilities, she resolved to endure the interrogation and return home to her children.

Before her group left home, women who went before her had schooled her on how to conduct herself. They said non-oath-takers suffered as much as the oath-takers.

Similar to police interrogations, officials punished, tortured, and insisted a person lied until the person, hoping to get relief, admitted he or she took the oath. Her advisers said the trick was to confess before the interrogators beat her senseless. They also said lying did not matter as long as one told her story with conviction.

When Mother's turn came, she had her story ready.

Two underfed, scrawny constables in khaki uniforms and elongated maroon-colored hats fetched and hustled her into a dimly lit cottage. She found two Gîkũyũ men, dressed in trousers, shirts, and overcoats.

Gîkũyũ-speaking officials, conversant with Gîkũyũ traditions, myths, beliefs, and the oath process, conducted those interrogations.

This became crucial during the Mau Mau era when the colonial government classified the Gîkũyũ Community into categories:

The masses whom the colonizers conquered and now destabilized yet again and herded them like sheep into guarded villages in the native reserve or European farms, segregated them in towns, or sent them to detention camps.

Political activists - the educated activists like Kenyatta, who engaged and believed in change through newsletter campaigns, reason, peaceful negotiations, and appeals to the English civil society.

The Mau Mau nationalists – the hot-heads, who emerged and became defined after World War II; most of their leaders were war veterans. They seethed with enthusiasm, choosing to live as a free people or die fighting for their birthright.

If the British could force them to fight and die in the thousands for someone else's country, they could surely fight for their own country; restore lands to their rightful owners, and expel the British from Kenya.

The nationalists complained those educated elite activists wasted time organizing, negotiating, rubbing shoulders with colonialists, and even traveling to London to "beg for their own lands" in the British parliament.

How could anyone negotiate the return of their own seized and occupied lands in the occupiers' country? Mau Mau members and their supporters and sympathizers marveled.

The loyalists – the middle-class Christian men, educated by the missionaries, and who sided, aided, and abetted the colonizers.

Through their education and religious affiliations, they educated their children, some of them abroad, and benefited socially and financially through colonialism.

Many of those loyalists owned sizeable pieces of land, and some of them had even turned into surrogate colonizers. Independence for their fellow Africans, therefore, meant more people to share with, which would have jeopardized their privileged lifestyles.

As a result, anyone who opposed or interfered with the colonizers' set hierarchy became an enemy of the loyalists.

So, after the Mau Mau uprising and the threat seemed serious enough for the colonial government to pay attention to, the loyalists, already with a stake in the system, became natural colonizers' allies and their power grew exponentially.

The colonial administration promoted the pseudo-colonizers to home guards, chiefs, and other senior positions with subordinates at their disposal.

The government also supplied the men with guns that enabled them and their rank and file to apply whatever heinous methods they could to ensure the Gĩkũyũ masses conformed to the colonial dictates, and that the Mau Mau got defeated.

The captured/defectors collaborators who came from captured ex-Mau Mau senior members. The colonial government spared these captives' lives for their cooperation.

The men's guerrilla warfare skills and knowledge of Mau Mau's operations and oath knowledge made them more valuable alive than dead.

Mother faced those types of loyalists at the screening cottage.

One official stood nearby while the other interrogated her. She told the interrogator she had never taken Mau Mau or any other oath. Except for basic questions and verbal intimidation, nothing else happened during that first stage.

Mother did not say how many rounds of interrogation she underwent. But for her last round, the constables marched her into a similar cottage where a white inspector (No African reached the level of an inspector in the colonial system.) came in during the session.

Just like before, Mother denied she had taken an oath.

One man slapped her.

"Get your story straight," he said, "otherwise you'll end up in detention."

When she stuck to her denial, the man slapped, shoved, and gave her two lashes. She ended up on the floor.

"I saw stars," she told two women. "No man ever hit me like that; not even my husband."

"As I lay there, an image of my children flashed through my mind. I realized it was the right time to confess. So I told them I had taken an oath just once. I talked fast and promised to tell them everything they wanted."

"Get up and sit on that chair," one interrogator told her. Mother struggled over a barrage of insults. Finally, she sat on the wooden chair while one interrogator rained questions on her.

"Describe how you saw the oath administered and how you took it."

The white inspector watched from several feet away.

Not having taken an oath, Mother described the process she saw Baba and other men follow to slaughter goats. She said the oath administers instructed her, along with others, to eat raw meat like animals.

"The interrogators had to know I was lying," Mother said to her friends. "I couldn't describe something I never witnessed."

She told her story so well, she said, that the white inspector thanked her in Kiswahili for her "honesty."

He cleared her of any wrongdoing.

Mother returned home on the sixth day.

Chapter 32

Passbooks

At the interrogation camp, Mother and her colleagues never learned what happened to their village-mates until the authorities whisked them into a van for their night trip back home.

Sometimes the officials cleared someone, but the person remained at the camp, likely waiting for colleagues to get cleared.

The cleared also never learned what happened to the ones from the neighboring farms with whom they shared cottages.

At home, we learned that a handful of male detainees from two of the farms never returned to their families. People said the government must have hustled them to detention camps.

To our relief, my parents and their fellow villagers all came out "clean." But that did not mean they felt secure or left the farm freely.

Throughout Kenya, the colonial government issued passbooks to Gĩkũyũ men and women, from teenagers to those a step away from the grave.

Passbooks contained columns, similar to booklets that post offices and banks used to record customers' deposits and withdrawals.

To walk to the market or the clinic, or anywhere else outside the farm, the law required every adult to carry a passbook showing the name of the farm, the farm owner, and his authorization.

David and Simon received their passbooks at sixteen.

"I received a passbook," Simon said, "and paid taxes before I could get an ID card."

He walked 20 miles to Nakuru town four times in two months to get his passbook. The man in charge—a Gĩkũyũ loyalist—subjected Simon to two rigorous interviews because he claimed Simon was not who he said he was.

He received his passbook on his fourth trip only because the loyalist was absent that day.

It could have been easier if Baba took Simon to Nakuru. But Kamunge said it was unnecessary because Simon was already a part-time employee on the farm, and Kamunge did not want two employees absent.

To Kamunge, Simon was mature enough to walk that far and negotiate his passbook, but not grown enough to receive his own monthly wages. Instead of paying him, Kamunge gave it to Baba for safekeeping.

During his four trips, Simon did not have a place to spend the night. Even if he did, he could not take a chance in case a white person or the police stopped him without official travel authorization.

He found it safer to walk back home and duck into the bushes if he heard a car approach.

Simon had reason to get nervous. Every white man in Kenya was an unofficial officer of the law. He could stop any African in public and ask for travel papers. If he deemed the papers flawed, he had the right, legally or implied, to arrest and deliver the individual to a police station.

(White women could have done the same, but because most of them were homemakers, they merely deferred to their husbands.)

Sometimes European men, mainly farm managers, slapped and kicked the so-called criminals they arrested before taking them to the police station.

Others, like the manager of neighboring Major Stein's farm where my cousins' families lived, did not involve the police. They dished out whatever punishment they deemed fit the "crime,"—which included physical attacks followed by warnings.

Word reached us that a man resisted, and it broke into a fistfight.

Those sadistic managers were a terror to young African men.

*

Although my life revolved around my mother, way before we moved to the village, I somehow understood Baba held the power and had the final say in our household. I believed he owned our homestead, our garden, the open grassland, his goats and chickens, and our belongings.

Then came our hurried move to barely unfinished hovels at Kabati and, after four months, on to the village while Mother complained in her usual self-talk. But Baba went along and remained quiet.

Initially, it confused me why he let all those changes happen to us just because Kamunge said so.

I saw and overheard enough throughout my seventh year to understand that although his authority loomed large in our homestead, it did not extend far to the outside. He owned little, and what he owned could disappear at the whim of Kamunge or his son, Kang'oro.

It's not that I thought seriously about these matters; it came to me as an awareness, which became clearer during the interrogations when unknown people came and whisked my parents away at night. I then realized with dismay that anything could happen to my family and Baba lacked the power to prevent it.

*

As my family and others settled into village life and to their new reality, including dusk-to-dawn curfew, news reached us that Kamunge wanted to appoint Baba as a "home guard." My heart swelled with pride.

I did not know who home guards were or what they did. But whatever they did, I believed, had to be powerful, which would elevate Baba to a higher status.

Although I lacked details then, it meant Baba would learn how to shoot a gun, receive a bonus, and be exempt from the higher taxes charged to regular Gĩkũyũ men.

My siblings and I waited for Baba's big day. None of us expected him to tell us when he got appointed. So, I observed him for any changes or mannerisms he displayed.

In the interim, if someone mentioned Baba's potential appointment, Mother clicked her tongue and continued with whatever she was doing without saying why.

"Your father will be Kamunge's eyes and ears," she said one day after she came from the hydrant outside the gate. She said this with an attitude, working faster, which made dishes rattle. Somehow, she knew something I did not know.

Negative energy oozed from her whenever she had no say in a decision Baba made. Whenever she got to that state, my siblings and I shut up and stayed out of her way.

I wondered why Mother could not be happy for Baba.

But I disliked anybody who talked about me to my parents. This meant if my father became Kamunge's eyes and ears, he would report people because, unlike Kamunge, he lacked the power to do much else. Then he would not regain or increase the powers as I had imagined.

I could not decide which was worse: being a home guard or being powerless.

I did not have to bother figuring it out.

My family waited and waited. Nothing further came up about the home guard position before we forgot about it and moved on to other village experiences.

SICKNESS

&

HEALTH

Chapter 33

Massages

We heard constant news about the Mau Mau and the colonizers' forces fighting. And a plane dropped leaflets to warn people against the Mau Mau. I recall picking up a flier, which had an image of a shackled man in dreadlocks, but I did not know what it said.

People went to jail, mainly men, for breaking curfew when they sneaked somewhere for a quick errand without authorization and got caught.

The news did not bother me because my parents never got themselves arrested. And except for David and Simon, who attended school, and Joseph, who went goat herding, the rest of us stayed at home.

Mother stopped taking me to her job or to the garden since we moved to the village. I now babysat Morry while Tabitha and Gîthũi stayed with me in our courtyard. I missed the time spent with Mother without my siblings' distractions.

Now, we had to adhere to her rule not to loiter outside our courtyard. But she allowed children—well-raised, she said, from specific families—to come and play with us during the day.

The four children who joined us came with their younger siblings, who ranged in age from three to four years.

Unlike me, who had to feed and carry my brother, the older children did not have to carry or take breaks to feed their younger siblings besides take them back home to eat in the afternoons. But I took it in stride, and not once did "poor-me" feelings cross my mind.

Meanwhile, Mother embraced village life. She quickly made friends who helped her in times of absences or sicknesses, like when Wanjeri came to cook for us during her interrogation hiatus.

I had not met Mama Alan yet, but I considered her my mother's friend. Mother referred to her with deference, as if she were a special grandmother to us. As I gained more freedom to go on errands outside our courtyard, I learned everybody revered Mama Alan and treated her with respect.

She and her husband, Mũgono, were the oldest people in our community. They lived outside the village, near the gate. Without the benefit of books, the couple, particularly Mama Alan, was a walking library for Gĩkũyũ's old ways.

They also served as surrogate grandparents to the village children because none of them (except for the Alans) had grandparents. They were dead, or a handful had joined the exodus to the *native reserve.*

Mama Alan flourished in her grandmotherly role according to rumors that reached me, which later proved true. She also gave massages to sickly children of mothers who sought her free service.

But her husband, Mũgono, a stooped, grumpy old man, with tufts of thick woolly hair as white as one of Baba's goats, did not cherish his grandfather's status, least of all to non-relatives. He directed his energy and respect toward his wife, who was also the conduit between him and their mild-mannered only son, Alan, and his family.

(Alan was the man who marched to the lorry stop during the exodus and ordered his daughter to return home and forget the lorry ride and her husband, Werũ.)

Contented to spend his old age in peace, Mũgono detested children who caused a ruckus, or hung around his homestead, hoping for snacks Mama Alan dished out at random. When he saw the children, he made garbled grunts and shooed them away with his walking stick.

"Get out of here," he said. "Go play elsewhere."

If Mama Alan caught him in the act, she chastised him and said children going to a person's homestead was a blessing. He never verbally contradicted her, but he continued his mean ways behind her back.

The day I first met Mama Alan, my brother Morry had cried nonstop no matter what our mother did. She abandoned cooking supper, sang him lullabies, walked him around half-slung on her shoulder, rocked him, but the boy never quit crying.

Mother diagnosed him with a bellyache, wrapped him with a towel, and carried him in a sheet she tied over her shoulders like a hammock. She invited me to accompany her to Mama Alan's house.

The invitation pleased me because it was the first time I accompanied my mother since we left Kĩrĩma-inĩ. That was also my first time to venture outside the village gate.

It was almost dark when we arrived at the small mud-walled, grass-thatched shack yards away from Mũgono's thingira. Before Mother knocked on the wooden door or identified ourselves, the door creaked open. Mama Alan appeared, stooped over before she hung onto the door and straightened herself.

"With those cries," she said, "I could tell a sick child is on the way."

I stood beside Mother, transfixed. I had not seen before such a leathered and wrinkled skin or such a serious stoop.

She wore a couple of necklaces and several bangles, but no earrings. Her holed earlobes dangled twice the size of Mother's.

When we entered, she offered Mother a low bench, but none to me. I sat on the dirt floor next to my mother, folded my knees, chin on top, hugged my legs, and watched.

The inside of the small house was warmer than I ever remembered ours, perhaps because I came from cooler air outside.

Mama Alan returned to her seat in front of a slow-burning fire.

Mother repeated her bellyache diagnosis.

"I'll take care of that," the village matriarch said.

She spread a gunnysack on the floor beside her, then fetched a small leather bag that contained knick-knacks. She felt inside and pulled out a small gourd, shook it, and placed it by her side.

"Let me have the child," she said as she rose and extended her arms.

Mother handed over Morry, who kept up his screams, although his voice sounded hoarse. He already displayed strained veins down his temple and brow.

Mama Alan laid Morry on the gunnysack and unwrapped the towel while he screamed and kicked. She took off his little shirt and handed it to Mother.

"Young lad," she said. "You'll get healed in no time. Where does it hurt? Here? There?" she asked Morry as if she expected him to answer while she pressed spots on his tummy.

I wished I dared to say, "He cannot talk yet. He only makes *ma-ma-ma sounds.*"

Mama Alan shook the small gourd again and squeezed a dab of oil onto her left palm, rubbed her palms, then spread them near the fire. When the oil got warm, she massaged Morry's belly in a circular motion. After several rounds, she reached to his back several times.

She replenished and warmed the oil two other times.

By the time she finished work on his midriff, Morry's screams had turned into intermittent whimpers.

She started another round from his head, shoulders, arms, and fingers, and on down to his thighs, legs, feet, and toes. Soon Morry's whimpers trailed off, and he fell asleep. Mama Alan wrapped the towel back around him and handed Mother her child.

*

Several months after Morry, I suffered a bellyache. Because Mother did not know how to massage yet, or believed her touch could not heal as well, she took me to our masseuse.

When we arrived, Mama Alan directed me to the gunny sack. But instead of taking off my dress, she rolled it up to my chest.

As she massaged my belly with the warm oil, smooth calming sensations overwhelmed and dulled the pain. My eyes struggled to stay open while my body relaxed into a state of euphoria where I longed to remain.

Against protests from every cell in my body, Mama Alan slowed her hands and stopped. She then ran cursory massages over my face and arms, to remove oil from her hands.

I wished she could give me a similar treatment to Morry's, but she gave only little children full-body massages.

On our way home, Mother held my hand to steady me while we walked about two blocks. When we arrived, I felt so lethargic I skipped supper and went straight to bed.

Chapter 34
Modern Convenience

Mother seemed to adjust to village life faster than anyone else in the family. She slowed her hectic pace and made friends. She also learned about bottle-feeding from her new network.

So far, for the first year of his life, Morry had accompanied her to her job or the garden. She either strapped him to her back or sat him close to where she worked.

During that period, she never took me to her job to babysit because I was still too young to walk the now-longer distance.

To put me back to work and ease her burden, Mother put Morry on a bottle.

Henceforth, she left him with me, did all her daytime business, and later returned home to find Morry and the rest of us alive and well, at least most of the time.

Morry and we, his siblings, dropped his milk bottle anywhere in the house or courtyard, only to grab and stick it in his mouth when he cried. When his food ran out, we chewed our food into a smooth paste and fed it to him as mother birds do.

Morry became the first child in my family to remain with younger siblings before Mother weaned him from breastfeeding. He was also the first to feed on milk bottles and eat food from surrogate mouths. All of us, older than him, accompanied Mother to work and suckled till age two.

The only problem, every few months Morry caught a disease that resisted Mother's or Mama Alan's oils and determined hands.

The disease baffled Mother because, according to her, my siblings and I never caught colds or such diseases before we moved to the village.

Whenever the mysterious disease struck, she fussed and said her child might die. The fear of one of us dying troubled her until we grew strong enough to withstand the attacks.

The first time the mystery hit, Morry threw up from both ends of his little body. Mother rushed him to the clinic at Njeki's Shopping Center. Francis, the Luo medical assistant, and the lone medic, considered it serious enough to refer her to Nakuru General Hospital, twenty miles away.

Since our area bus left for Nakuru town only once a day, Mother waited until early the following morning. To sustain Morry overnight, she gave him teaspoons of water-like solution that Francis gave her.

She and Morry spent a week at the Nakuru General Hospital, that first time. They stayed a week each of the other two times he fell sick within that year.

I failed to understand Mother's concern and worry about death, something that sounded alien and beyond my imagination.

So far, her absences were the ones that troubled me.

Every time she and Morry returned home, he looked as healthy as one of those baby images featured on baby food cans. The entire household rejoiced. We took turns playing with him. Those of us who could handle his weight bounced him on our knees. Those not strong enough played peekaboo or mimicked his baby talk.

I recall looking at him and thinking I had never seen him that healthy. Maybe the sickness and hospital treatment did him some good.

After those hospital visits, the medics prescribed a bottle of clear water and gave Mother a new baby bottle to replace the old one. They also issued her packets of powdered milk.

The healers failed to appreciate that the modern conveniences they promoted to mothers did more harm in places like ours without clean water, indoor plumbing, or bathrooms.

For years, they remained ignorant that the free bottles they issued to mothers after hospital visits were the source of some of those diseases.

If medics and European farmers could not figure out that peasant African mothers needed to breastfeed—because they lived under different circumstances from European mothers—how could Mother and other village women know?

Even when the medics knew, they never disclosed what ailed a person. Perhaps they hated to share their hard-gained knowledge or believed peasants too stupid to understand.

So, Mother never learned what Morry suffered from so she could take precautions.

But Morry pulled away from the shadow of death. In between germ attacks, he grew older and eager to emulate the rest of us.

He tossed his bottle aside and reached for a mug even before he could hold it steady. From his insistence, Mother or any of us helped him with the mug until he got the hang of it.

Today, I wonder whether Morry's sickness pushed Mother to become a home remedies activist when she relied on them more and more.

Chapter 35

Dentist

During Morry's poor health, the rest of us remained healthy. But a year later, my family started on the road to sickness that preyed on us for the next five years. It attacked us one at a time, sometimes in twos, and finally, almost the entire household.

But David and Simon, in their early teens, never fell sick. David went away to boarding school after one year in the village, so he did not count. But it made little sense that Simon never became ill.

I never associated sickness with Baba because he never got sick except once in my mid-teens that I know of. He caught a cold, groaned, and moaned lest the household became too busy and forgot his distress.

But for the rest of us, Mother included, ill-health never trailed far from us. To curb the maladies, my parents turned into avid shamans. Well, maybe they were all along, but I noticed it between ages seven and eight.

They used our homestead as a makeshift mini-hospital, staffed with a self-styled doctor, nurse, and dentist, with a distinct division of labor.

Baba, the dentist, provided free dental services to the villagers who sought them. No one in our family cared for his archaic dentistry; we kept our dental issues hidden from him.

But the adults who came to our courtyard to seek his treatment became so grateful. Besides lack of money to visit a clinic, they did not have to miss a day from work.

When a patient suffered a toothache, all night long, as each claimed, he or she came early in the morning before Baba left for work or on his weekend errands.

A patient, usually a man, shoulders hunched, resting his achy jaw on his palm, shuffled into our courtyard with one or two men in tow.

The patient and his helpers headed to *thingira* where operations took place.

The men made an impromptu appointment, and a brief consultation followed before Baba fetched his surgical gear—a sisal sack and a pair of pliers. He spread the sack on the living area floor, instructed the patient to lie on his or her back, and the supporting staff to take their positions.

"Open your mouth," Baba said. "More! Open wide!"

He then went to work.

Depending on which tooth ached, after several attempts, amidst sighs and grunts, Baba raised the pliers with the culprit lodged in its jaws for all to see.

One time, a molar proved so stubborn that Baba needed the handlers to get more vigilant. The two men restrained the patient—one held his legs down, the other his midriff. Whenever the pain became excessive, the patient jerked this and that, and when he failed to escape his captors, he increased his guttural noises. Despite the dentist's and his helpers' efforts, however, the molar remained lodged.

"The tooth seems welded into your gum," Baba said.

He withdrew his pliers, and the men released their hold.

"I don't want to dislocate your jawbone."

"Do whatever you can," the patient said, as if his mouth were filled with mashed potatoes.

"I can't take a chance with your jaw."

"I didn't sleep a wink last night," the patient said, now seated hunched, his palm to his jaw. "It was like a drill digging into my jaw."

The men kicked suggestions around.

When they resumed, Baba held a screwdriver.

He pried the sides of the man's tooth. Then he laid the screwdriver aside and took the pliers.

By then, the man roared like one of Kamunge's bulls in heat.

We children were up and about before Baba could remove the stubborn tooth.

Because of the ruckus the patient caused, we now huddled and watched, standing at one side of *thingira*'s doorway. Baba focused on his task so much that he did not notice us. When he finally raised his pliers with the culprit's molar wedged between its jaws, we scampered away toward nyũmba.

*

I do not recall when my milk teeth started loosening, but definitely after we moved to the village. I felt a sensitivity whenever my tongue tripped on one of my bottom front teeth. Soon, a sharp pain assaulted my nerves whenever my tongue or food touched the tooth.

My mind remained fresh with two horrors that villagers endured under Baba's hand. I shuddered when I imagined a pair of pliers digging into my mouth. No way would I let his hands come close to my ailing tooth.

I kept my pain a secret.

In time, when food or tongue touched the tooth, I twitched or made an ouch sound. As the frequency of the snappy, sharp pain increased, the burden of my secret became unbearable. I told Joseph in confidence.

But our family's comedian and reporter could not keep such a hot item to himself. He spread the breaking news to the entire household.

That evening, Mother asked me to let her test whether my tooth had loosened enough to come out. I shook my head and walked a few paces toward the door. I could not trust her with my tooth. I had witnessed her trick Joseph once. With her forefinger and thumb in his mouth, she wiggled his tooth and, without warning, pulled it right out. Joseph yelped and whimpered.

"You didn't say you'll take it out!" he said.

"It was too loose," she told him. "If I left it, you would have twin teeth."

Her twin-teeth classic threat went beyond my imagination because I had seen no twin teeth yet.

In my case, Mother left my tooth alone. She did not fool me—I knew her ploy to mark her time until she figured a trick to get her fingers into my mouth. She could not even help herself from adding a warning to my tooth worry.

"If it becomes too loose, it'll fall out, and you may swallow it with food."

But Joseph, having gone through several tooth evolutions, shared his wisdom.

The following day, my tooth remained a major topic in our courtyard. Joseph, already gone goat herding, could not help me carry out his previous night's advice.

It was now up to my younger siblings and me and a couple of village children to debate and decide on the best way to remove my tooth.

We dismissed Baba's dentistry outright.

There remained two options: first, let Mother pull my tooth. Second, use the newest method Joseph schooled us on that he either devised or picked up from village boys.

I had already turned Mother down. So, I remained with only Joseph's method.

Tie one end of a string around my tooth and tether the other end to a post. Then snap my head backward and my tooth would snap the other way.

It distressed me to think about it.

After much anguish, I resolved to wait until my tooth became looser.

Nobody said more about the matter and I thought it settled.

But David, now fifteen, had come home from boarding school. When we moved to the village, he stayed one year—the specifics I recall little of—and then left. He seemed several rungs above us in shoes and clean clothes and hardly said a word to me unless he addressed all of us.

Now, he sat on a stool close to the granary from where he watched us go on and on about my tooth, the first best image I recall of him.

"Wanjirũ," he called me. I turned toward him, surprised.

"Come closer," he said. "I'll help you assess how long the tooth will take to loosen."

Assess sounded reasonable.

Six feet from him, I opened my mouth and touched my ailing tooth. I slightly wiggled it. "Look," I said.

"How long do you think it'll take?" he asked.

I hesitated. *How would I know that*?

"I don't know," I said.

"Can I feel it?"

I inched closer to my brother, my plan to protect my tooth forgotten.

"Eeee," I said, my mouth wide open.

"Is this the one?" David asked as he touched each of my loose tooth's two neighbors.

I shook my head slightly.

The second my brother touched the shaky tooth, he gripped and yanked it out in one swoop.

"Ah!" I said in surprise and a flash of sharp pain.

I cried and cried. Not out of pain, but because of the tricky way he removed my tooth.

Subsequently, I never mentioned my wobbly teeth to anyone. When their time to depart my mouth came, their roots loosened and loosened, and finally rotted. My tongue periodically nudged the old crowns outward while the new teeth inched and pushed upward. Finally, the poor rootless crowns tipped over and dislodged.

Maybe my siblings used the same painless tactic because, after everyone's permanent teeth settled in, I noticed one of Simon's old canines failed to tip over. It scooted slightly up his gum and latched onto the outside of its replacement. He ended up with fraternal twin canines on his upper gum.

To my credit, and the rest of the family, I never asked or mentioned Simon's twin teeth ever. And for consolation, Simon remained well while the rest of us got sick.

Chapter 36

Treatments

Besides dentistry, Baba foraged for herbs and dug medicinal roots around the farm's woody areas when he went to set or check on his beehives. He returned home with about two or three feet of branches and various sizes of roots tied in a bundle.

At home, he separated the herbs for general wellness from those for treatment. He then removed nodes and scraped off loose bark, and cut the branches or roots into six to eight-inch sticks, which he tied into small bundles with sisal strings. Afterward, he gave the bundles to Mother, which she stored in the granary.

Whenever Baba slaughtered a goat, depending on the type of herb he needed, Mother boiled one bundle and strained the liquid. Or Baba grated the herbs into the soup with a blunt knife. Then he whipped the soup using *kîbîrî* or *kîbîri*—whipper—a wooden whip made from a finished skinny wood fitted with a dried goat's vertebra at the tip. He whipped the soup until it foamed.

Some herbs turned soup flavorful while others turned it bitter.

Herbal soups supposedly treated and strengthened the drinker's immune system; the bitterer the soup, the more effective. My father was especially diligent about those soups after Mother gave birth. I overheard her and other women say that soups reset a new mother's bones and stimulated milk glands.

I noticed that Baba put certain herbs into the soups that he drank or shared with other men. I never thought it unusual or tried to learn the names of those herbs. Neither did I think to ask what the herbs healed or protected.

I now understand there were herbs that older men used, and still use, from shrubs or barks of trees like *mũiri*, an indigenous tree in Kenya. These are to guard against enlargement of prostate gland or prostate cancer.

For health maintenance, the men drank "tea" made from dried *mũiri* leaves once a day. If it was for treatment, they drank it twice or three times a day. Some drank it straight, and others added a little honey to lessen the bitterness.

Nowadays, I'm told by one herb drinker, some men spike it with lemon and honey.

Mũringa was the other tree men used by drying and grinding its bark into powder. They drank a teaspoon, or equivalent, of the bitter liquid a day for maintenance. A man doubled or tripled the intake if he fell sick. One could alternate *Mũiri* and *Mũringa* treatments.

*

While Baba used herbs for health maintenance and sickness prevention, Mother used them to treat her whole brood when more than one child sneezed and developed a runny nose.

She cut a variety of leafy branches and tied them into a bundle like a broom. Then she boiled water in a big corrugated iron basin and dipped the bunch into the boiling water with the handle sticking out. She turned over the leaves several times, and the fumes caused her entire house to smell like a hospital dispensary.

When she determined the vapor was most potent, she placed the steaming basin at the center of the living area. She then arranged low benches around the basin and told each of us to sit there.

Aware of Mother's occasional drill, Gĩthũi inched away from the group.

Unconcerned, Mother brought a blanket, sat on the highest stool, and threw it over the rest of us. She then covered every sliver of light that sneaked through so no steam escaped. It turned pitch black and as hot as a sauna.

She told us to bend slightly toward the basin. Some of us complained about the heat, others asked whether we were well yet.

But our family's stubborn child insisted he was not sick and remained on the outside, his empty little bench on the inside. Amidst our chatter, we heard him walk about.

"Are you hot?" he asked at intervals. "Are you burning? Are you done?"

It was hard to know what situation bothered Gîthũi more—freedom and loneliness or captivity and our company.

But he did not remain indecisive for long before his FOMO—Fear of Missing Out—pushed him closer and closer to the igloo.

Mother took him by surprise when she raised the right side of her blanket, grabbed the six-year-old by the shoulder, and tucked him next to her like chickens do to their stray chicks.

"This vapor will travel through your nostrils," Mother told him, "and burn the cold."

"I don't have a cold to burn," Gîthũi said before he gave up on his half-hearted struggle.

Mother turned the leaves every so often and more swooshes of hot vapor assaulted our faces.

When a turn of leaves produced very weak heatwave, she said, "We are all done!" and threw the blanket off.

This brought excitement as we shrieked with bravado. It was hot and yet we braved it, we said. Even Gîthũi had the nerve to exclaim twice, so we heard him.

"Even me!" he said. "I did it!"

*

Mother believed treatments failed only when she did not know what a child suffered from.

But after a group's treatment, sometimes the well remained well, and the sick continued to swipe mucus off their noses with their backhands.

Mother claimed the cold would have gotten worse without treatment.

But if the cold persisted, our family's *doctor*, nurse, and performer of a hundred other jobs—titled and untitled—had an answer for that.

"A mother with children," she said, "shouldn't knock on doors at midnight seeking treatment."

Her goal, she said, was to ensure we did not develop pneumonia or infect others.

So, Mother stocked her pharmacy in her bedroom and replenished it when it ran low.

When a cold became stubborn, she lathered the patient's chest with Vicks VapoRub and put a dab in each of his or her nostrils.

In case of a non-mucus complaint, she felt the patient's brow with her backhand, then felt the chest with her palm to gauge how fast the heart thumped.

"I think it's pneumonia," she announced.

Based on her diagnosis, each of us had caught pneumonia.

If she ruled out a stubborn cold and claimed one suffered from pneumonia, she augmented Vicks VapoRub's treatment.

She started a three-times-a-day regimen of MB, a white round tablet at least four times the size of an aspirin. I presume she got those tablets from Francis, our trusted medical assistant, or she bought them in Nakuru town.

For babies, she quartered the MB and split it into halves when a child grew older.

She put the half or quarter in a spoon and ground it into powder with the back of another spoon. She then added a little water, stirred, and fed it to the patient.

For a cough, she prescribed a tablespoon of golden Cod Liver oil once or twice a day, depending on the seriousness of the cough.

Whenever I endured a tablespoonful, I washed my mouth afterward to lessen the taste and smell. But occasional teensy smelly belches escaped and plagued my throat for the duration of the treatment.

Sometimes Mother forgot and continued the regimen even after an individual stopped coughing.

Chapter 37

Hybrid Treatments

There were no clinics in Solai when we moved to the village. If people fell sick, they traveled on a bus to Nakuru General Hospital, twenty miles away, an entire day's trip through a rugged dirt road.

To fill the void, Memsahib, Kamunge's daughter-in-law, opened a "clinic" at their huge equipment barn, about 50 to 100 yards from their colonial house.

She cleaned and bandaged wounds and treated village children's minor ailments.

But Mother did not seek help because she believed she could treat us just as well.

"I don't care for tiresome explanations," she said.

But she had no choice one Sunday, several years before we moved to the village. I was a toddler and Tabitha a baby.

Because it was Mother's market day, she awoke at the first rooster's crow at about 3:00 a.m. She first packed what she needed for her trip. Then she lit a fire, cooked porridge, and kept it aside for the children.

Joseph, still young enough to spend nights at nyŭmba, heard the noise and left his bed. In the living area, he found

Mother making tea. Now fully awake, he went and retrieved his ugali from the corner where Mother kept it for him the previous evening. He sat on one side of the fire pit across from Mother, who held Tabitha in her lap.

Mother cooled half a mug of tea for Joseph and handed it to him. After he took the mug, he shifted to get comfortable. The small stool he sat on wobbled and gave way. He fell on his side and his left arm ended up in the fire. Mother thrust Tabitha down and rushed to rescue Joseph. During the rescue, his arm's skin peeled off.

The homestead erupted into restlessness when the commotion awoke the sleeping. Mother left David and Simon to mind Tabitha and me and, instead of going to the market, she and Baba walked the four miles to Kamunge's compound while she held the screaming almost-five-year-old.

Fortunately, the arm burned only on the outside and Joseph could rest it on Mother's shoulder.

Kamunge's two German Shepherds announced my parents' arrival. Exhausted, Joseph produced hoarse whimpers while veins bulged on his brow and temples.

Memsahib received details of her patient from one of her domestic workers during her morning tea. After she finished, she walked to her clinic and invited my parents in. As a numbing agent, she gave Joseph a packet of sweets while she attended to his burns. Whenever the pain distracted him and he stopped munching, she encouraged him to stuff more sweets in his mouth.

Over the years, whenever Joseph talked about the burn incident, he told the sweets-only part. Even we, his family, never paid attention or mentioned the leathery scar he carried on the length of his arm.

Other than Joseph's incident, we never suffered wounds except for scrapes and scratches that healed without intervention.

For troublesome stomachs of babies and young children who cried but couldn't explain what ailed them, Mother became our masseuse instead of asking for free service too often. But she never reached Mama Alan's skill level.

I recall her applying oil on my face and arms. I felt the roughness of her callused hands, unlike Mama Alan's soft hands that got too old to work the land besides her tiny vegetable garden.

When we contracted diseases that massage could not cure, Mother treated us instead of walking four miles to the clinic at Njeki's Shopping Center.

I learned of the clinic, or the authorities built it, about two years after we moved to the village. With the new clinic, despite the distance and a charge, villagers abandoned Memsahib's free services.

Besides a cleaner, Francis treated patients alone in the two-room structure for years before the health department employed a part-time assistant for him.

Several years later, the government hauled into the yard a small two-room trailer on wheels for when they did vaccinations.

In a rare case of constipation, Mother kept a bottle of castor oil she bought at Patel's General Store. Solai grew plenty of *mbarîki* (Ricinus communis) plants with lots of seeds from which factories made castor oil. But nobody bothered our *mbarîki* plants. They grew and multiplied.

People could have chewed the seeds, with the same results, I suppose, but nobody did.

Although I do not recall using the castor oil treatment, my youngest sister, Wairimũ, wished she could when mother used a never-seen-before treatment on her one Sunday afternoon.

Mother cooked us a late lunch when Wairimũ, at about four years old, sat tilted on one side, quiet and listless. She watched the rest of us chatter as we waited for our first major meal of the day since our morning porridge. She started to whimper and walk about without saying anything.

"What's wrong with you?" Mother asked.

"My poop won't come out," Wairimũ said right there in front of everybody. Now that we all knew her secret, she whimpered, and in a minute her lips pouted and quavered.

Mother rushed to her "pharmacy" only to find that she overlooked to replenish her castor oil. With none of my brothers present to send to Patel's general store, I expected Mother to send someone to borrow the oil from our neighbor. But she had no time to waste. By her quickness, we could tell a novel idea had come to her.

Within a minute, she raised Wairimũ by her armpits, rushed her behind the granary, and laid her in a fetal position on the grass. She then rolled Wairimũ's dress to the waist that left her little bare bottom sticking out.

Mother's index finger went to work.

It pried marble-size hard balls from Wairimũ's backside while she let out a series of tiny sobs. She hushed as soon as the crude colonoscopy ended.

After the treatment, Wairimũ disclosed she had eaten a heap of *kĩmande,* maroonish seeds shaped like split peas that contained lots of fiber. Instead of chewing the seeds, swallowing the juice, and discarding the bulky fiber as we did, Wairimũ swallowed everything.

She never touched those seeds again, even after we instructed her on the proper way to eat them.

Mother treated eyes, too. When my baby sister's or brother's eyes got sick and swelled, Mother let the baby finish breastfeeding. She then patted the baby's eyelids, pointed her nipple, and squeezed drops of milk into the eye. In days, the sickly eyes cleared. She did the same to my baby brothers' penises.

We asked her why.

"It'll help it open so he can pee properly."

She had a cure for labored breathing, too. When an infant suffered clogged nostrils, Mother sucked the snot from its nose and spat it out. Yuck!

Although I said nothing at the time Joseph paraded around without a shirt on, I thought my parents' treatment had gone too far. I noticed four razer keloid scars about an inch each on his left ribcage.

No one spoke of it then or ever, but I suspect Mother or Baba bled him when he developed high fever or pneumonia. That was Mother's default ailment.

With us getting sick one at a time, Mother looked like a wizard. She prescribed treatment or took a patient to a doctor and within a week—Poof!—the disease disappeared.

But she lamented, fearing her brood might succumb when the Big Two hit back-to-back.

Chapter 38
Predatory Viruses

A virus or a germ attacked our household, usually one child at a time. But one time, someone—nobody learned who—caught *gĩthũkũ* (measles). Then the disease spread until all six of us children fell under its spell. Mother had to stay home to nurse her patients.

"I can't take you to the hospital," she said. "They don't know how to treat measles."

Even Francis? Her favorite medical officer? I thought he could cure any disease.

When Mother said the hospital could not treat measles, she remained the only person we could count on. We lived and thrived based on her knowledge and actions.

She fussed and stressed because we not only refused to eat, but she also lacked a magic cure.

"A child needs to eat something to fight the disease," she said.

She insisted we eat.

At one time, she brought little pieces of scrambled eggs to my mouth like a baby. I shook my head. She coaxed me to take one bite. I tightened my lips and turned sideways. Even the smell of it caused my diaphragm and food track to convulse.

Was *Ngai* punishing me because of my eggs' greed? The time I wished I could fall sick so Mother could feed me eggs? And now I could not stand their sight or smell?

Besides chicken, which we considered a special meal because we rarely ate it, and when we did, given our large family, one piece each was not enough to satisfy our palates, eggs were the other delicacy that fell in that category. My siblings and I hardly ate them unless we fell sick.

Although Mother could have spared a couple of eggs for an-out-of-village visitor like other village mothers, but we had no visitors except for when grandmother Nyandia came to see baby Morry and even then, I doubt she would have expected or cared for eggs.

We could have eaten eggs in Kîrîma-inî if the focus was not on goats, but we owned few chickens at the village and they could not lay enough eggs to hatch new chicks and leave some for the family.

And because eggs were easier to sell, Mother sold the extras at the market to buy what she, like other mothers, considered necessities like sugar and cooking oil.

But it did not matter that Mother spared some eggs when we fell sick; we did not want that type of "treatment." If she could not feed us to starve the measles, however, she turned to the next alternative to help us heal faster.

She washed us with Baba's homemade beer and gave us a sip after every wash. The taste, I recall, was like that of a smooth Chardonnay.

Measles affected all of us the same way, but, unlike my siblings, my right eye remained shut for weeks, or for how long the measles ravaged our bodies. Mother worried I might become mono-eyed. Perhaps to reassure herself, she parted my eyelids every day and checked. Like a lot of rural mothers, she sometimes spat on her finger and brushed off boogers from my eye, which I detested especially now that I was almost nine, albeit a tiny nine.

In my case, for a reason I never learned, Mother did not prescribe breast milk drops for my eyes. She took a last look at my right eye after I healed and announced it only had a *njereri* (a floater). I did not know what she meant by njereri. So I did not concern myself with it; I saw as well as before.

But during a routine check-up when I grew up, my optometrist said I had a scar on my retina. And although I did not pay attention until decades later, my eye ended up "lazier" and never saw as clearly as the left. Was measles the cause of that, too? I'll never know.

*

Measles left gradually the same way it had sneaked on us. Mother glowed when she saw us go outdoors.

"A child who doesn't play is sick," she used to say.

We soon engaged in our activities and she declared us cured.

Within the month, however, while we sat around the fire, she looked at Joseph and said the measles left him weak. We all turned toward him. Every part of his uncovered body parts looked ashy with lines of scratches.

In two days, Tabitha and I started itching and scratching, and Gîthũi soon joined us.

Mother said we suffered from *mũthandũkũ* (chickenpox).

Soon the itches became so severe we too scratched and left ashy streaks all over our skins. Meanwhile, tiny pimples sprouted throughout our bodies and even inside our mouths. They became larger by the day and some developed into big bumps.

Mother said not to scratch, no matter how much our skins begged.

"If you scratch," she said, "you'll have scars for the rest of your life."

The rest of my life meant nothing to me, but I made efforts to follow my mother's wishes. At times, however, my resolve broke and I sneaked satisfying scratches behind her back. I suppose she expected it because she monitored us.

Whenever she saw any of us wince and wiggle, she called out.

"No scratching!"

But chickenpox did not devastate us as much as the measles. We could still move about in the courtyard and out of Mother's sight. It became harder and harder for her to keep an eye on us.

When an area itched excessively, I tightened my body. If I failed to get relief, I rubbed my palm over my dress, until the itchy wave passed.

Mother restarted her beer regimen. Because the disease attacked from the inside, according to her, the beer therapy stimulated pimples to the surface. The more the bumps sprouted, the faster we would heal, she said.

The back-to-back sicknesses so overwhelmed Mother that she stopped or forgot to evoke, "This disease will kill my children" that she indulged in back in the damp hovels at Kabati and during the measles attack.

In a week, the bumps filled with fluids. Even if we did not scratch, some bumps ruptured when we sat, rubbed on clothes, or slept. They left open sores, which dried and became scabs. When they healed, they left scars like any other wound. But the bumps that remained intact dried like aged skin and finally flaked and fell off.

I'm not sure how long chickenpox dotted our bodies, but when we started playing—a sign we had healed well enough—our bodies displayed spots like those of a cheetah.

Gĩthũi's spots came out the biggest, some the size of a dime. Mother said he would carry scars for the rest of his life. But, as his body filled out, the spots disappeared.

That was the last time my family fell sick as a group.

Chapter 39

Lethal Bite

Family sickness may have interfered with Mother's work schedule, but the household's rhythm remained unchanged. She took care of the sick and her other chores despite the stress and worry she shouldered.

She and Baba even got together between Morry's hospital trips, as we soon learned.

When Morry turned two, and I eight, Wawerũ came along—another boy for me to babysit.

But as good mothers did, mine had already trained me as a well-rounded peasant girl. So, after months of taking Wawerũ to her job, she put him on a bottle and left him with me like she did with Morry. Taking care of him all day long posed no strain on me.

On my way to nine, I played house with other children with my baby brother strapped to my back. We picked weeds to imitate coffee cherry pickers at the scrubby bushes that grew between our granary and my parents' garden that they established next to the fence.

I jumped and skipped while I carried Wawerũ. The only time I asked another child or Tabitha to help me hold him was when my turn came to play hopscotch or jump rope.

Just like with Morry, when Wawerũ cried when his food ran out, we chewed our food for him. But if milk ran out, or before Mother cooked something for him when she returned, whoever held him shushed him by sticking his or her tongue or a lower lip into his mouth.

That did not fool him. He fussed until he got what he wanted.

*

Although Mother seemed indestructible, things changed and showed our family how crucial she was to our lives.

Her journey to sickness started with a trip to the garden to cultivate and get vegetables. When she returned, she said something bit her ankle.

"I was pulling weeds under dense bean plants," she said, "when I felt a sharp prick."

"What was it?" Gĩthũi asked, young enough to butt into adults' conversation and in Baba's presence.

"I don't know."

"You didn't check?" Baba asked.

"I let the pain pass," she said. "But when I brushed aside the plants, I saw nothing."

"There're lots of insects this time of year," Baba said. "Could it have been a wasp?"

"My mind tells me it could've been a snake."

"It's hard to tell."

"It broke the skin."

Except for Gĩthũi, none of us children said anything.

Mother then turned to her evening chores. By supper, her right foot looked fatter and smoother than the left, but not bad enough to alarm my parents. They would decide in the morning if the leg became worse, they said.

When I awoke, Mother sat by the fire pit making morning tea, her fat leg outstretched over a low bench somebody must have helped her get. The leg looked shiny, like a giant puffed sausage.

She remained seated and sent us to fetch whatever she needed to make our breakfast.

We eyed her, confused and subdued.

I am unsure whether Baba asked Kamunge for transportation on the tractor-drawn wagon, but Baba lamented that the bus had already left for Nakuru.

Late afternoon, when he returned from work, Mother labored to breathe and she spoke with difficulty.

Baba sent for Francis—the medical assistant at the clinic at Njeki's Shopping Center. Still in his white coat, clutching a black doctor's bag, Francis walked the four miles to our house.

When Francis appeared at the door, the entire family relaxed.

Mother trusted and believed in his diagnosis and treatment as a follower would a cult leader. She also liked that she could speak with him in Kiswahili, unlike at the big hospital where she relied on nurses to translate English for her.

"You can't be sure 'sisters' always tell you what the doctor says," she once told her friend when they talked about the cons of the *big* hospital.

Francis gave Mother a shot. He said not to bother going to Nakuru General Hospital because they used the same antivenom.

Mother had stayed for too long without treatment. As a result, she remained bedridden for days and days, and Simon, then fourteen, gave her a washrag bath twice. He also did house chores and cooked for us.

My siblings and I never saw our mother during that period. Our only contact was when we heard her voice when she grunted, asked for help, or gave instructions to Simon.

Then one mid-morning, when my younger siblings and I played in the courtyard, I heard Mother's voice. I turned toward the porch. She lay on the ground, leaning on her elbow, and Simon stood beside her. He seemed unsure of what to do.

As I gathered, Mother got tired of staying in bed and asked Simon to help her go outdoors for some sun. Somehow, Simon got her off the bed.

"I think leaning against the granary would be better," she said with difficulty.

"That's too far," Simon said.

"I'll try to get there."

Mother crawled an inch at a time and sighed as she dragged her half-covered log-size leg. Simon remained beside her and walked a small step at a time.

The leg looked bigger, smoother, and shinier than when I saw it last. She took breaks in between, leaned on Simon, and then resumed her crawl.

Halfway to the granary, she tried several times to reach out and push herself forward, but she did not move an inch.

Finally, she gave up.

"Getting to the granary will take me all day," she said, her breathing labored.

She struggled to push her body to a sitting position. She could not do that either. Her body looked lopsided. Besides, the humongous leg weighed too much for her to move.

She planted her elbow on the ground, supported her head, and asked Simon to get her a stool or a chair for her to support herself.

While Mother struggled, my younger siblings and I watched from afar, where we now stood between the granary and the goats' cottage since she appeared on the porch.

The huge leg scared me. I had not seen a snake by then, but from my parents' description, I feared a snake may have slithered and wedged into her leg. And worse than that, I resigned myself to having a helpless mother who crawled.

She craned her neck with an effort and looked at our miserable group.

"*ũĩ*! *Mwathani*," (Oh, Lord.), she said, softly. "My own children are afraid of me."

We said nothing or changed our stance; our eyes remained glued on her.

Simon brought a folding wooden chair. When he unfolded it, Mother raised her torso and hung her elbow onto the chair while Simon pushed the chair little by little toward her. Set, she basked in the sun.

I doubt she got comfortable because she tried to shift and failed several times. Her face looked flushed and strained because of the tropical sun.

She stayed about ten minutes before she asked Simon to help her crawl back in.

*

As Mother struggled to manage our household through Simon, nobody mentioned the hospital again. Francis had taken care of it and that was that.

Gradually, Mother improved to a point she could crawl outdoors by herself, without Simon keeping guard.

Baba must have felt confident about her recovery to tell his snake story.

One late afternoon in Kîrîma-inî, before I was born, Baba walked from the courtyard to his *thingira*. When he reached the threshold, he heard rustling, likely after something he carried touched the rafters.

The instant he looked up, a spray of liquid hit his open eyes. He cried out in pain and groped to the entrance. By the time somebody answered his call, the snake that I now guess was a cobra slithered away.

Baba sent one of my half-brothers to report to Kamunge and get some medicine. My half-brother returned with a little bottle of eye drops.

Even with the anti-venomous drops, Baba's eyes remained swollen shut.

After two weeks in that state, he became desperate and lamented.

"How will I earn a living as a blind man?" he asked. "Kamunge will eject me from the farm. Where will my family go?"

He lived with that misery for an entire month.

Then slowly, the swelling subsided, and his sight gradually returned.

"Don't worry about your mother," he said. "She'll heal just like I did."

That made me happy. Things always turned out as Baba said. It meant I would not get stuck with a mother who moved about on her knees.

As Mother's leg healed, the swelling subsided to where she could hobble and support herself by holding onto a wall or doorway, and rest without putting weight on the leg. Baba made her a wooden crutch to ease her hobble.

Meanwhile, her leg skin, from the hip to her foot, started peeling like snakes shed their skins. By the end of the second month, her leg displayed brand new skin like a newborn.

Chapter 40

The Surrogate Mother

After Mother healed from her snakebite, our household rhythms returned to normal. I looked at her illness as incidental and forgot about it.

But within the year, perhaps after six months, she complained of a throbbing pain on one side of her ribcage. She winced if she moved. She could not even sleep on that side. Her breathing became increasingly labored.

Just like before, Simon picked up cooking, which proved Mother's serious condition.

Because she could not walk, Kamunge donated his tractor-drawn flatbed wagon to take her to the bus stop. Baba never mentioned the agony she must have suffered during the three miles along the dirt bumpy road or the 18-mile bus ride to Nakuru General Hospital.

Late afternoon, my heart sank when Baba entered the courtyard alone.

"The doctor said your mother needs to remain in the hospital," he said.

Did the doctor say how long? I wondered. I hungered for more information. But Baba said nothing else.

My mother's ill health worried me, and I hated how it had disrupted our household's routine and rhythms. But what I hated the most was Mother's absence; I looked after Wawerũ day and night.

Somehow, news reached me that a woman in the village said perhaps Mother's body retained snake venom residual. I did not dwell on it. Women liked to talk and sometimes made unfounded claims.

Although I perked my ears to catch their gossip whenever I could, the women's assertions meant little to me unless my mother concurred.

Baba proved helpless and of no help to us, yet again. Unless he asked a question or wanted one of us to fetch him an item, he did not deal with us in Mother's absences. He also never brewed or drank beer.

Whenever he returned home from work or the garden, he came home and checked on the goats. After he saw them safely in their cottage, he cooped up in his thingira.

If someone dropped by, Baba said, "The children's mother is away." He never said where she went unless the person asked.

I now believe he wanted them to know he could not offer them tea or food.

At suppertime, when Simon or someone else took food to Baba, he asked, "Have the children eaten?"

*

As if Mother's sickness did not weigh on me enough, my youngest brother, Wawerũ, a toddler shy of two years old, fell sick. He refused to eat or drink anything during the day.

I tested him by laying my backhand on his brow. Next, I put my palm on the left side of his chest. Based on his brow's temperature and heart's rapid thumps, I concluded he suffered from a serious illness. I guessed pneumonia, but I did not say.

"Wawerũ is sick," I told Baba when he returned from work. "He threw up and his heart beats fast."

Baba came close to where I held Wawerũ in my lap, his head on my chest. After he observed him, Baba left and returned in about an hour.

The following morning, he did not leave for work. Instead, he did something I never thought he could do. He took Wawerũ to Nakuru General Hospital.

At nine years old, I went to assist him.

At the hospital, after the doctor checked Wawerũ, he talked to the nurse. She translated to Gĩkũyũ what he said in English.

"The doctor says your child is too sick to return home," she said.

What's the doctor going to do? Take him to Mother? jumped to my mind before I heard the second translation.

"He has admitted both of your children."

After my surprise wore off, and the grownups settled the matter, I wondered what it would feel like to sleep away from home. I did not feel fearful, abandoned, or sad.

My father assured me that the hospital would take care of my brother and me before he left. And, at nine, I did what my parents told me without question.

Besides, Mother—my main anchor in life—languished in one of the hospital's wards. Perhaps someone could show me where they kept her.

I also did not forget that the doctor admitted me as the surrogate mother to my little brother, which, in my mind, meant I needed to represent my parents well.

To my relief, the nurse took Wawerũ from my lap and put him astride her hip. He rested his head on her shoulder.

"Follow me," she told me.

By then, Waewrũ had remained strapped to my body for 21 miles, three of which I had walked with him on my back.

We walked through a corridor before we left that building and entered a children's ward lined with cots on both sides. The mothers with little children sat beside the cots or held the children in their laps. Some older children, whose parents could not stay with them in the hospital, turned toward us and looked with sickly subdued beady eyes.

Halfway inside the ward, the nurse deposited Waewrũ into a baby cot that he and I would share during our hospital stay. The side of the cot reached about three feet high, lower than the ones of our woven bed that I shared with my sister Tabitha, which was so high it had an entrance like a treehouse.

Whether the hospital fed me or what I did that evening, besides dozing off, is lost to memory.

Chapter 41

The Hose Incident

I could climb in and out of our hospital bed without difficulty. But when Wawerũ's health improved, he stood inside the cot and the railings reached up to his chest. A quiet child, he never tried to get out; instead, he hung onto the railing and waited.

Because my arms were not strong enough to bear his weight, we both waited for a nurse.

Nurses put no diapers on him, so the two of us awoke every morning with our gowns drenched in his urine. Most times, a nurse wiped him with a damp washcloth. She then gave me a gown and asked me to change while she dressed him.

On two or three occasions, with nobody to remind me to pee before bedtime, I dreamed of going to the toilet and added to the drench that guaranteed our trip to the cold shower room.

Every morning, two nurses—patients called them "sisters"—came in. They dressed in light blue or green uniforms with white caps atop their heads. One pushed a big bin, and the other dragged a smaller cart with clean bedding and tie-back gowns.

I saw this only when the nurses reached our cot, and one of them shook me awake. Otherwise, unlike at home where my body knew when to wake up, I would have slept through the stench and breakfast.

When the nurse woke me, I got out and stood by our bed. I raised my toes because the cold cement floor hurt my soles and a chill ran up my legs. The bin nurse lifted Waweru and put him beside me and he bunched his toes. He looked disoriented, his little gown crumpled and barely covering his bottom.

The nurse then stripped off the wet sheets, threw them like discards into the big bin, and wheeled it to the next cot.

The second nurse remained behind to tidy up and take us to the shower for our daily wipes. Before she took us, we waited while she wiped the thick green plastic wetting sheet that protected our mattress and made the bed with fresh sheets.

At home, we did not bother with cleaning as nurses did. With dirt floors, urine got absorbed and its smell got mixed with the chickens' and goats' smells. We scooped poop off the floor or from wherever it landed with velvety leaves called *maigoya*.

I now wonder how Mother stayed clean when she shared her bed with a little one. But when she weaned each of us— like on a conveyer belt—we moved from her bed to ours. Then the last two children distracted her. From then on, the rest of us urinated in our beds without fuss. It was almost dry by the next bedtime.

This went on until the stench reminded Mother her children slept in filth. She rounded us on a Saturday and told us to spread our bedding to dry over the stick fence or on the grass behind the granary. Nobody bothered to put up a clothesline.

Once in a long while, Mother washed the rags that passed for our bedding.

*

One night, Wawerũ outdid himself. I woke up, and, while rubbing my eyes to orient myself, the stench assaulted my nostrils. I turned my head down. The sight and odor of our two bodies made me cringe.

Urine and feces covered us from the rumpled gowns down to our feet. It embarrassed me that Wawerũ's behavior exposed the backwardness of our family and shamed my parents in front of the clean, well-dressed hospital people.

That was the first time I realized that my family did not measure up, and that I needed to keep that part of our lives hidden.

"Oh! These children!" the nurse said the minute she laid eyes on us.

She scrunched her nose, narrowed eyes to slits, and shook her head in slow motion. She then stretched her arms and lifted Wawerũ from his armpits. His soiled bottom and legs dangled as she hustled him toward the shower room.

"Follow me!" she said to me in haste.

Confused, Wawerũ let out muffled whimpers.

Instead of washing Waweũ using the plastic basin half-full of water like she did, or letting me wash, the nurse deposited him at the center of the shower room.

"Stand by your brother!" she ordered me.

She pointed the hose at us and opened the spigot. She hosed us with cold water while she stood at a distance, slightly bent so the filthy water would not spray her.

Waweũ cried his throat hoarse. He grabbed my arm to shield himself from the spray. I pulled his body beside mine so he would not slip and fall on the slippery cement floor. I released him when the spray stopped, and he could stand without the danger of falling.

He stood with his little fists clenched. His body trembled from head to toe while his front teeth—the only ones he had—gritted as his lips vibrated and produced a humming sound.

I shivered, too, but held tight, willing the ordeal to end.

The nurse punctuated the routine with an occasional click of her tongue until she dried us. She then thrust a gown toward me while she dressed Waweũ.

I thought we deserved it—the only time I recall ever thinking I deserved poor treatment.

After all, I reasoned, she is not our mother.

Fortunately, a warm breakfast awaited us. They usually fed us porridge with milk or cocoa milk and bread with lots of butter.

Chapter 42

Hospital Nuances

Each morning, a medic stopped at our cot and read notes on the clipboard that hung on the wall. He gave Waweru medicine and noted it on the clipboard before he continued to the next cot.

Twice during our stay, a group of medics came and held a discussion right there by the cot. Their leader checked Waweru, and they discussed some more before they moved on to the next patient. They stayed longer at some cots than others, especially at the older children's cots. But, besides getting information from the nurses, they never spoke to the children.

A white woman visited the ward at random. She wore a white dress, a belt snug on her midriff, white shoes, and a sturdier white cap with colored stripes, unlike the plain ones the other nurses wore. She talked to the nurses, stopped at a patient's cot, or gave instructions.

Patients called her "Big Sister."

Whenever Big Sister entered the ward, nurses concentrated on their jobs without talking to their colleagues, and, if they said anything, they talked in low voices. Big Sister acted in charge and gave instructions or asked questions.

One morning, she came with the male white doctor and the two went from bed to bed, checking on patients. They reached where Waweru and I stood by our cot, waiting for our nurse to finish making our bed.

While the doctor read notes on the clipboard, the Big Sister told our nurse to place Waweru back in the cot. The doctor then did his usual routine—listened to Waweru's chest and back with a stethoscope.

Afterward, the two—the doctor and Big Sister—remained by our cot while they talked in English, a language I had never heard when I arrived at the hospital, but by then I had learned it was white people's language.

When the two turned their backs and moved a distance from us, a nurse close by snapped her chin toward them.

"What diseases are they saying she will catch?" the nurse said softly in Kiswahili. "There are diseases right here."

"If I were in charge," our nurse said, "I'd let these children visit their mother."

I had noticed that the nurses talked among themselves in Gĩkũyũ and spoke in English with senior personnel. They used Kiswahili with people who did not speak English or Gĩkũyũ, or if they wanted to conceal information from non-Kiswahili speakers.

As a nine-year-old Gĩkũyũ girl in the mid-fifties, I doubt the nurses expected me to speak or understand Kiswahili. But I did, although I do not recall when I learned the language. It must have been when my family moved and encountered non-Gĩkũyũ people who lived outside our village.

Tugen men dropped by our household to consult Baba about work, and I probably picked up the language during those interactions.

By my hospital stay, we had lived in the village for three years already.

I felt kindly toward the two nurses because I knew if they had the power, they would let me visit my mother.

Based on the work the doctor and Big Sister did, and how timidly the others behaved around them, I concluded they held the power. But they seemed so far removed from me I expected no special treatment from them.

Even if they did not let me visit my mother, I felt grateful to the hospital people who cleaned, made our bed, fed us, and treated Wawerũ.

I even excused the dress-imitation silly hospital gown they issued me. The wide neckline slid and exposed my right shoulder. I let it hang where it reached—down to my upper arm—until it irritated me enough. To return the neckline back in place, I flipped up the crook of my elbow occasionally, like one suffering from a shoulder tic.

Because I had no chores and did not carry or feed Wawerũ, but only sat with him when he became well enough to join me outside, it turned out a vacation for me.

I frolicked or skipped around the yard during the day. But because the other children were too sick to play, I never got into any body-stimulating activities.

I enjoyed gawking, watching, and listening to mothers talk about their families and their sick children. They said their husbands visited them on Sundays only when they were off work.

Occasionally, amid my play, I talked to children around my age who became fit enough to venture outside but not strong enough to play. Between talking to the children, mealtime, and listening to grownups, I never felt lonely.

And because most, if not all, mothers spoke in Gĩkũyũ, like in my village, and my mother was in one of the hospital wards, I never missed home either.

Although most late afternoons, I looked at the women and a sharp whiff of loneliness stubbed me, and I longed to see my mother. I then stopped whatever I was doing and looked around the buildings' landscape, and wished I knew in which ward they treated her. I could then sneak in for a minute and visit her.

I mulled over the thought for a moment before I realized such a daring venture went beyond my capabilities.

Sneaking with adults all around me felt so daunting. I doubted they would let me loiter around the wards and perhaps get lost.

Baba came to check on us the following week. A nurse must have told me because I do not recall seeing him.

I can only surmise that he did not know the ward they put us in, and he had to wait in the hospital's main waiting area. When he finally got someone to direct him, he found Wawerũ asleep, and me outside. A nurse gave him an update, and then he rushed to visit Mother before the visiting hour ended.

Before Baba returned a second time, however, the doctor and the Big Sister came to our cot again. The doctor checked Wawerũ while he and the Big Sister talked back-and-forth while our regular nurse stood aside and waited. As usual, the doctor wrote on the clipboard.

After they finished, the Big Sister talked to our nurse in English before she and the doctor walked to the next cot.

"The doctor said your brother has healed," our nurse told me in Gĩkũyũ. "Your parents can take you home."

I indulged in a moment of joy before reality dawned on me.

My mind churned.

Does she mean we leave today? I wondered.

Yes, we could leave. I heard Mother and other women say bus conductors never charged a child my age or younger unless she occupied a seat.

But could I stand and hang onto a seat frame with Wawerũ on my back when the bus reached the bumpy dirt road?

Perhaps a woman will offer to hold Wawerũ, or the conductor will give me a free seat.

But would he let me travel alone with a toddler?

If he does and the bus drops us at the Solai Road bus stop, I can walk the two miles home.

But I do not know my way to the bus stop in town.

Perhaps Big Sister will let a nurse take us.

I recall feeling lost because I knew my thoughts and wishes led nowhere. I never expected the hospital to release us without Baba.

I doubt hospital personnel knew Kamunge's farm location where they could find my father. If they recorded patients' "addresses" at all, they used the names of the farms where those patients worked.

Although it was beyond my capacity to think that way, I did not know the real name of my father's employer or the farm's name—people called it gwa-Kamunge (Kamunge's farm). I now accepted with dismay that my brother and I would remain wards of the hospital, at least for a time.

But I should not have worried myself because, although the medics stopped Wawerũ's medical treatment, the nurses treated us the same as before. We ate, slept, waited for Baba, and I thought about my mother.

Chapter 43

Instant Relief

Good food and treatment, and no chores, did not dull my craving to return home, the need of which heightened when someone reminded me.

"I thought doctor discharged these children," a nurse said while she stood by our cot.

I flipped an evil eye toward her as my little chest contracted.

"We are waiting for someone to come for them," our nurse said.

Each day, I felt embarrassed, as if my brother and I were intruders.

At one time, a woman in a group seated outside asked me:

"When are your parents coming to get you?"

"Baba?" I asked, as if everyone knew my family's plight.

The woman gave me a withered look.

"I don't know," I said.

"Where is your mother?"

"In the hospital."

The women exchanged glances and comments about "the poor children." None of them asked me about going home again.

Standing at the side yard, where patients who could go outside spent most of their daytime, I looked over the short shrubby fence at each man who walked by wearing a hat and coat, hoping it would be my father.

Although I could see an average man only from the chest up, I knew I would recognize him if he appeared.

I did this routine for days, maybe a week, and wondered whether Baba got too busy and forgot about us. Then both of us would turn wards of the hospital permanently.

I had heard Mother and women familiar with hospital culture say that some families dumped their very sick and never returned.

I did not think Baba would abandon us. Perhaps he just got too busy. I had not figured he could only come on a Sunday, the only day he did not go to work.

Finally, I saw a man amble toward the hospital buildings from a distance. I squinted and looked as usual. My mind thought I recognized the man. I squinted some more in case my eyes tricked me. Closer and closer, I saw it was really my father.

Great relief rose within me. It turned into excitement. I balled my fists, put them next to my cheeks, and watched until Baba disappeared inside.

Besides wait for the nurses, I wondered what to do next.

To unsettle me even more, the two nurses who took care of us and knew our plight did not come to work that day.

I remained in limbo for a long, long time—perhaps half an hour. The waiting ravaged my insides.

Then a nurse came.

"Your father is here to get you," she said.

I said nothing. I did not know what to say.

The nurse lifted Wawerũ, and I followed her.

She had already hung our miserable clothes—a dress, a shirt, *ngoi*, and a piece of cloth—on the cot's railing. After we changed into our clothes, she secured Wawerũ to my back and led the way.

We found Baba in the waiting room.

"*Wĩmwega*" (how are you), he said.

"*Ndĩmwega*" (I am well), I said.

"How is your brother?" He bent over to look at Wawerũ.

"He got well."

On our way to catch the late afternoon Solai bus, Baba said:

"Your mother is already at home."

"Is she healed?"

"Yes. She's healed."

The news made me so happy I could not wait to get home. From that minute, I keep not a single memory of our trip home.

*

Mother rushed out of nyũmba when she heard Baba's voice.

"My children are home!" she said when she saw us.

She unloaded Wawerũ from my back and placed him astride her hip.

I experienced instant relief that I still recall. Similar to our trip to the hospital, I had carried Wawerũ on my back one mile from the hospital to the bus stop and two more miles from our bus stop to our homestead. And he remained strapped to me even when we rode on the bus, unlike before when I carried him only around our courtyard.

Mother straightened and adjusted Wawerũ's shirtsleeves and collar.

Wawerũ looked up at her quizzically, turned toward me, and reached out.

"Have you forgotten me?" she asked. "It's me, your mother."

"He's not sick anymore," I said. "He can walk okay."

She kept him on the ground.

He reached and tugged on my dress, but determined not to carry him again that day, I took his little hand and put it on Mother's dress and told him, "this is Nyacuru."

Meanwhile, I relaxed knowing our household would not be as lonely as when I left. And Simon and Wanjeri did not have to cook for us anymore; I preferred Mother's cooking.

As soon as I sat down for Mother to give me food, my siblings bombarded me with questions. They sat close to me as if they envied me for having gone on such a long safari.

I told them about my bus ride, how *makanga* handled luggage, and even the musical honks the driver played to alert passengers before the bus reached a bus stop. I described jacarandas, and Nakuru town and its clean people, the nurses and doctors I encountered, the mothers with sick children, and every hospital experience that I could remember, including the buttered bread.

I skipped the entire episode of the cold-water hose and my two nights' accidents. Joseph would have had a fun season with that one.

I wanted to wow them, not make them laugh or make fun of our embarrassing behavior.

It was my first time to glow under such limelight. I sensed and believed I had matured into a big girl and that my parents could trust me to behave the right way in their absence.

Chapter 44
Mother's Hospital Story

Mother stayed in the hospital for almost two months and returned home three days before my brother and I arrived.

Two women came to visit her the next day. They returned the following Saturday with three others who carried loads of firewood on their backs. Two of the women arrived with water in big metal containers—there were no plastic containers yet—and food, cooked or uncooked, in kîondos.

This was a Gîkũyũ custom (which endures to this day, although it has become commercialized and sometimes includes men) that they called *itega* (baby shower) when women visited after the birth of a child. They carried supplies to help the new mother until she regained her strength and to see and welcome the baby. A woman or two also helped similarly when a woman fell sick.

Now I wondered the reason the women arranged *itega* for Mother while she had no new baby, and she looked fine to me.

Whenever women came, Mother made tea while they socialized. Unlike before when she complained the visits wasted too much time, she now took time to tell the women about the sickness—at least the part she knew—that landed her in a sick ward.

When she went to the hospital, she said, one side of her torso pained so much she could hardly walk. The doctor admitted her so he could run some tests.

After the following day's X-ray, the doctor said liquid pooled in her ribcage. He never specified whether the liquid pooled in her lungs or somewhere else.

In the operating room, the doctor made an incision through Mother's ribcage. He sucked with a syringe more than half a small bowl of slimy liquid.

He repeated the same routine a week later.

Besides Mother's sickness, the women traded stories about hospital abuse.

Because their stories were hearsay, they wanted Mother to tell them her experience, perhaps out of curiosity and, most likely, to confirm their secondhand accounts.

During those exchanges, I learned that although Mother went to the hospital sick, she gave birth to a baby boy. But she returned home alone.

That intrigued me.

What happened to the baby?

"The children are around," a woman warned Mother when she reached that part.

"What are you doing here?" Mother would ask me. "Go out to the other."

Sometimes I got lucky when Mother called and sent me to get an item. After I took whatever she wanted, and the women seemed too engrossed in their talk to notice me, I scooted at the side and sat on the floor, my legs folded, chin on my knees, quiet.

I wondered why Mother went to the hospital to get a baby. She got her children at home, with the help of a midwife or two.

During the three births I recalled, I remained confused about where babies came from. First, I believed the women brought the baby. By the third birth, I wondered where those women got the baby themselves. I agonized about it before I accepted that was unknowable. I needed to wait to learn about it when I became an adult.

But the women's stories about hospital births held my curiosity. I eavesdropped enough to get a cohesive story.

When Mother went to the hospital because of a throbbing pain in her ribcage, she was also pregnant.

After about a month, and when she still nursed her ribcage, she went into labor. When it intensified, the nurses took her to the labor ward or birthing room.

The room came with one of those narrow OBGYN beds, like an examination table—only higher—on which they birthed babies, at least in Nakuru General Hospital.

If a prospective mother did not pay attention, she would end up three feet down on the cement floor, Mother said.

But a doctor and a midwife or a nurse usually stood on either side of the bed, ready to scoop the new arrival.

In Mother's case, she said, there were two nurses—perhaps a midwife and a nurse. She did not know the difference because medics did not introduce themselves in those days.

During the birthing process, one woman slapped Mother twice on the side of her bare bottom and accused her of failing to push as instructed.

"Call us when you are ready to follow instructions," the midwife said as she and her companion left the room.

"The baby wasn't ready to come," mother said. "Those mean sisters became tired of waiting."

In less than half an hour, Mother called out.

"Is there someone out there?" She asked. "The baby is coming!"

Her sporadic utterances went unanswered. Her other option was the bell on the wall several feet from the bed that the staff used.

The baby broke through and fell onto the bed. Because of the prolonged labor, it only whimpered.

Mother propped herself on her elbows. But if she reached for the baby, they would both tumble to the floor.

She screamed, instead.

On her second scream, the two women burst through the door.

One of them rushed to tend to the baby while the other rang the emergency bell.

The doctor soon arrived.

He put an instrument in the baby's nose and mouth and sucked out fluids. He then held the baby by his ankles and dangled him upside down. The doctor slapped and slapped the baby's bottom. But it was too late; birthing liquids had already reached the baby's lungs.

"I watched in disbelief as the doctor mishandled my baby," Mother said. "If I hadn't gone to that hospital my baby boy would be alive today."

"Ah!" one woman said. "I'll never step in a hospital to have a baby."

"Never again," Mother said.

I wanted to know more. Like, what happened to the baby? Where did he go? But as usual, I put that in the unknowable until adulthood category.

In those days, children never asked questions concerning adult conversations, especially when the adults did not expect them to understand or pay attention.

Parents wanting to protect their children from adversities their psyches were not ready for never informed their children of such occurrences.

Chapter 45

Mami

As Wawerũ grew healthier and older, he gave me the break I craved. He cherished his independence and required my attention only when he became tired or hungry. He played with the younger children and trailed the bigger ones, copying whatever they did.

He was not alone.

When my family moved to the village, over three years earlier, my siblings and I referred to Mother as "Nyacuru."

For the first year or two, no child claimed that addressing our mother by her name was wrong. Perhaps because we stayed in our courtyard and other children did not come around to play with us yet.

But when I turned eight, children started coming to our courtyard. I noticed none of them referred to his or her mother by name.

When I said, "Nyacuru doesn't want us to go outside our courtyard."

"Who is that?" They asked in chorus and scowled.

"Nyacuru!" I said, thinking the children did not understand me.

"That's your mother's name?" several children asked, and one or two paused and gave me a side-eye.

"Yes," I said, now puzzled.

Why did they behave as if my mother's name sounded funny or distasteful?

"What kind of name is that?" one child asked and giggled.

Before then, it never occurred to me that some names were unsuitable. They were just names.

But after I realized the children believed Mother's name "ugly," the mere mention of it embarrassed me. I quit saying her name in the children's presence.

Instead of saying "Nyacuru doesn't want you coming to our courtyard," I said, "You are not supposed to come to our courtyard."

When I spent time at the hospital, I noticed the children who could talk did not call their mothers by their names either. Each of them used the title "Mami."

To me, that confirmed the children in my village knew better than I did.

When Wawerũ and I returned home, I agonized because I still suffered a snicker or a funny look when I forgot and mentioned my mother's name.

It bothered me so much that my subconscious mind could not take it anymore.

One evening, Baba and Simon went honey harvesting at one of Baba's beehives. Mother cooked in *thingira* while my younger siblings and I sat around the fire.

In a second, a sensation I could not contain rose from my
chest and shot up my throat. It implied I needed to solve
Mother's name issue there and then.

"Mami!" I said in haste, to get relief.

Mother stopped her kitchen activity and glanced at me,
paused, then resumed her chore without a word.

"Mami" was what I heard children refer to their mothers. If
we were in Gĩkũyũland, I would have called her *maitũ*.

The change felt daunting. I did not attempt another "Mami"
that evening.

But from the following day, hesitantly at first, I started
calling her Mami. My siblings joined in, one by one, starting
with Gĩthũi and Morry, who did not even seem to notice the
transition.

When David returned from boarding school, he never
mentioned our evolution or respected it. He continued to call
Mother "Nyacuru." But one week before his one-month school
holiday ended, he switched to "Mami."

My mother became *Mami* for the rest of her life.

End of Book 1

REVIEW

Would you mind leaving a review about this book wherever you bought it?

If you got it from the author, you can leave the review through her website wanjiruwarama.com and click on the book link.

The review doesn't have to be long or detailed. The main thing is to share your opinion whether you liked the book. And if you did, what you liked about it. This helps other readers find the book and decide if it's worth reading.

Thank you,

Wanjirũ

wanjiruwarama.com

ACKNOWLEDGEMENTS

Many thanks to the West City Writer's Workshop members for the suggestions they offered and for cheering me on, especially the facilitator, Esteban Ismael, who listened and put up with my raw stories, saying they had potential.

To Timothy Calaway and Margaret Mckerrow for reading the manuscript in its early stages and giving me ideas to make it better. Thanks also to Mary Thorne Kelley, my cheerleader and proofreader who has been with me from the beginning of my writing career, you mean the world to me. And to Mary Tina Morgan for proofreading the manuscript.

To Editor Isabella Furth, Ph.D. whose structure suggestions made the book better and more reader-friendly.

To my late brothers: Simon Ndurumo Warama for clarifying and updating me on our family's history and quirks—this book wouldn't have been the same without him—and John Gîthûi Warama who valued my writing so much that he used the word "legacy" before he died; a poet in his own right who I failed to convince to write a book. Thanks also to my half-sister, Nancy Wairimũ Warama Mũriũki, for clarifying my father's rocky relationship with his children.

More thanks go to my Books Fan Club, friend Kathy Davis, and fellow writer Karl Keating for helping in cover choices, and to Leon Lazarus for his guidance on the mechanics of a user-friendly website so I can showcase the book.

And many thanks to you, the reader, for choosing to spend time with my words.

Wanjirũ

wanjiruwarama.com

Made in the USA
Las Vegas, NV
02 August 2022

52560466R00194